KU-501-037

PARENT SURVIVAL MANUAL

A GUIDE TO CRISIS RESOLUTION IN AUTISM AND RELATED DEVELOPMENTAL DISORDERS

Edited by

Eric Schopler

University of North Carolina School of Medicine
Chapel Hill, North Carolina

PLENUM PRESS • NEW YORK AND LONDON

Library of Congress Cataloging-in-Publication Data

On file

ISBN 0-306-44977-3

© 1995 Plenum Press, New York
A Division of Plenum Publishing Corporation
233 Spring Street, New York, N. Y. 10013

10 9 8 7 6 5 4

All rights reserved

No part of this book may be reproduced, stored in a retrieval system, or
transmitted in any form or by any means, electronic, mechanical, photocopying,
microfilming, recording, or otherwise, without written permission from the
Publisher

Printed in the United States of America

For all parents
who have successfully struggled
with the obstacles of autism

Foreword

T his book is the result of more than 30 years of experience and hard, resourceful work by Eric Schopler and his team—first as lonely pioneers, now as leaders whose influence extends as far as Kuwait, India, and Japan. It is the fruit of a concept so simple, human, and obvious that it is hard to believe that not so long ago it was both revolutionary and controversial. Parents of children in mid-adulthood well remember what it was like to be considered the cause of their children's problems, rather than part of whatever solutions could be achieved. In 1971, when Eric Schopler described us as our children's "cotherapists" in the *Journal of Autism and Childhood Schizophrenia,* it validated and strengthened the efforts we had already been making. When Division TEACCH began to develop new methods to help autistic children and—this is what was revolutionary—actually to teach them to parents, we could begin to heal.

So what seems, and should seem, ordinary and matter-of-fact about this book—that it is a collection of ingenious solutions that parents have developed as responses to the continual challenges of living with autism—feels to me more like a miracle. It is not only that its nine chapters provide ingenious suggestions for dealing with the difficulties that arise in every aspect of daily life with an autistic person. Each chapter illustrates the root principle of Division TEACCH: collaboration between parents and professionals. The staff of TEACCH have accompanied each solution with a commentary that analyzes why and how it works and relates it to more general issues of autism. The *Parent Survival Manual* is thus the work of parents and professionals together, in mutual respect and trust. That this is no longer a miracle, but something that we now have the right to take for granted, is the measure of how far we have come.

Clara Claiborne Park

Williamstown, Massachusetts

Acknowledgments

In all our TEACCH activities, we are indebted to the parents of individuals with autism whose cooperation and participation have given us new insights into the problems of autism. However, our indebtedness to parents in this volume is unique. Hundreds of parents and some professionals contributed interesting and informative solutions to behavior problems to share with other parents and interested professionals—in the form of 350 anecdotes. Some were contributed anonymously or retold by someone else. Some authors requested that their names be withheld. Accordingly, it is not possible to name and thank each of the parents individually. But we offer our thanks to all of them for their creative solutions. We thank them, too, in advance for the inspiration and help they have extended. The collaboration with such parents has inspired us to serve these children throughout our careers.

We also acknowledge with great appreciation some of the many TEACCH colleagues who have compiled and analyzed the various chapters. Marie Bristol was tireless in calling together groups of parents, especially at meetings of the Autism Society of America, the Autism Society of North Carolina, and the Autism Society of Michigan. She also reviewed and contributed to the chapters compiled and analyzed by Rhoda Landrus, Margaret Lansing, Lee Marcus, and Bruce Schaffer. All of these therapists contributed their insights and understanding of persons with autism and gave time despite the heavy demands of their TEACCH commitments. It is a special pleasure to acknowledge the contributions of Alice Wertheimer. She wrote about her experience as a parent and advocate in Chapter 9 and used her unusual dedication and compassion toward parental needs to compile the wealth of resources in that chapter. Ann Bashford and Vickie Weaver handled the typing and computer complexities with their usual competence, cooperation, and efficiency. John Swetnam and Christine Reagan provided initial editorial and technical assistance. Suzanne Orr completed with thorough efficiency the construction of the iceberg content for the chapters and much of the editorial preparation of the manuscript. Anthony Alvarez remained cheerful through the final editing stages. As one of our most experienced psychoeducational therapists, Carol Logie appled our unique TEACCH method of integration of behavior and cognitive theory to picture the iceberg metaphor as a useful teaching device.

The Autism Society of America, the Autism Society of North Carolina, and the Autism Society of Michigan also offered us special assistance in identifying both parent vignettes and community resources. We are grateful for their expertise and cooperation. The University of North Carolina School of Medicine and the North Carolina State Legislature make all our work possible in Division TEACCH of the Psychiatry Department. Finally, Eric Schopler sparked the idea for this volume almost 10 years ago. He underestimated the delayed birth process and is responsible for any editorial deficit that may have slipped through the fine networks woven by parents and colleagues.

Division TEACCH
University of North Carolina School of Medicine
Chapel Hill, North Carolina
April 1995

Contents

Chapter 3

Chapter 4

Chapter 5

Chapter 6

Chapter 7

Chapter 8

Chapter 9

COMMUNITY SUPPORT 179

Alice Wertheimer

1

Introduction: Convergence of Parent and Professional Perspectives

Eric Schopler

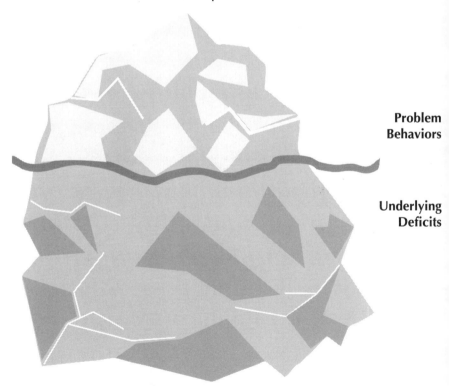

**Problem
Behaviors**

**Underlying
Deficits**

F irst awareness that the newest member of the family may have some special problems or delays with communication, social interaction, or other aspects of development can come as a shock with gnawing uncertainties. How long will the problem last? Will it affect learning, friends, or family relations? Is it mild or severe? What does it mean? Does it have a diagnosis, a treatment, and a cure? There are variations of these general concerns, questions as different as each family's struggles with its own unique challenges. Some questions can be answered by knowledgeable professional consultation. Others, often involving uncertainties of the future, are dependent on unknown circumstances and are difficult to predict. These are concerns shared even by parents of children without special problems. On the other hand, with the autism complications, these concerns can take some unique forms.

We have compiled this volume to make available our experience with these concerns and with the children who provoke such preoccupations. More important, we have been inspired by parents who have struggled effectively with the most daunting problems while at the same time searching for answers about the future. Their problem solutions were often ingenious, creative, and cunning. At times they discovered new understanding of their child from close and thoughtful observation. Sometimes they translated observations into new behavioral interventions, which were being simultaneously discovered by professional researchers. Experience can be the best teacher.

The anecdotes in this volume were collected over a period of 6 years at parent meetings and annual conferences of autism societies at national and state levels. During this period, we also conducted a survey to see what problems parents of children with autism or related developmental disorders found most troublesome. These included problems with aggression, communication, unusual behaviors and special interests, toilet training, eating and sleeping, and difficulties with play and leisure. Although these behavior problems were not all-inclusive, they were cited most frequently and appeared most often in the anecdotes that parents told to us.

Some anecdotes contained solutions that seemed like the best and only ones possible under the circumstances. For other problems, a somewhat different interpretation and approach might have worked equally well. We included some anecdotes because a parent was enthusiastic about the result, even when we might have looked for an alternate solution. We found all the anecdotes to be instructive, upbeat, and inspiring—inspiring because each family was coping with a special problem, one they did not ask for, cause, or deserve. Nevertheless, they had the energy and ingenuity to deal effectively and optimistically with their circumstances. Most of them also had some bad times when the feeling "Why me?" took up the child rearing space. But most of the time they made a good thing of it, like an oyster's pearl from an irritating grain of sand. These anecdotes can inspire others who are struggling with similar problems.

The purpose of this manual is to make these parental anecdotes available to the reader and to provide an interpretation of each anecdote with an emphasis on observing and recognizing the troublesome behavior, inferring the causal factor triggering the behavior, and then improvising an intervention or an environmental adjustment. This intervention should be humane and useful for the child, fit the lifestyle of the individual family, and reflect the best available information. Frequently, the rational processes underlying parental interventions are the same as the rational processes of professional therapists. It is our highest hope and expectation that the reader will benefit from our focus on the overlap between parental and professional wisdom, based on rationality, compassion, and good cheer. The anecdotes can offer specific suggestions for coping with difficult situations. More important, they will stimulate ideas for adapting solutions to challenges from your own child. We do not endorse the use of any particular intervention or anecdote, nor do we suggest that this be read as an alternative to professional help. We, of course, advise the reader to seek professional help with severe and/or dangerous behavior.

This introduction includes a definition of autism or the group of children referred to in the collected anecdotes. This is followed by the background to our collaboration with parents and professionals and the prioritizing of treatment techniques and principles. Finally, we explain the anecdotes, the contents of this volume, and how to use it.

We hope this provides you with a starting point for understanding and coping with some of your family's special challenges. As of this writing there is no known cure for autism and related problems, but there are ways of reducing each child's problems and fostering both development and learning. It is important for you to be informed about the state of knowledge at this time, but regardless of how much you read, the best knowledge is gained from experience with your own child. This manual is dedicated to those inspiring moments and to those who have shared them with others.

DEFINITION OF AUTISM AND SIMILAR CONDITIONS

Kanner (1943) is credited as the first to describe autism in the psychiatric literature. Some of the main features he identified have been supported by a substantial body of research and are reflected in the fourth revision of the *Diagnostic and Statistical Manual* (DSM-IV) of the American Psychiatric Association (1994). DSM-IV identifies problems in three broad areas: social interaction, communication, and stereotyped patterns of behavior or special interests. Twelve criteria are provided for these three areas. To fall in the autism classification, an individual has to show 6 of the 12 criteria, with at least two indicating social interaction deficits and one criterion in each of the communication and stereotyped patterns of behavior categories.

The four criteria in the social interaction category are as follows: marked impairment in the use of multiple nonverbal behaviors, failure to develop age-appropriate peer relationships, lack of spontaneous seeking to share interests and achievements with others, and lack of social or emotional reciprocity.

The five communication criteria include the following: a delay or lack of spoken language development (with no compensation through alternative modes of communication), marked impairment in conversation skills, stereotyped and repetitive use of language, and lack of spontaneous age-appropriate pretend or social imitative play.

The four criteria under stereotyped patterns of behavior include preoccupation with at least one stereotyped and restricted pattern of interest to an abnormal degree, inflexible adherence to nonfunctional routines or rituals, stereotyped and repetitive motor mannerisms, and preoccupation with parts of objects.

Besides meeting six of these criteria, the individual must show delays in either social interaction, communication, or imaginative play. The onset or first recognition of the condition has to occur prior to age 3. When these conditions for the autism diagnosis have been only partially met, the child may be grouped with "pervasive developmental disorder," Rett's disorder, childhood disintegrative disorder, or Asperger's disorder. The children referred to in the anecdotes throughout this volume have been described with at least one of these diagnostic labels.

Although the diagnosis provides an important description of the syndrome, it does not identify a number of learning characteristics that can offer obstacles to one child but not another. These can include problems of comprehension, verbal expression, attention, abstraction, disorganization, poor memory for nonspecial interests, and so on. Relative patterns of cognitive strengths have also been identified in autism. These can be seen in special interests, rote memory skills, and good visuospatial processes. Likewise, the social problems of autism have been studied in the form of problems with shared joint attention; attention shifting; social attachment; shared understanding; turn taking; ability to maintain a conversational topic; and ability to interpret social cues such as tone of voice, facial expression, intonation, and rhythm of speech. It is necessary to understand both the deficits and strengths of each individual child. It is equally important to understand the environmental circumstances under which these characteristics show themselves. For example, a teacher who uses a visual schedule can get a child's attention, while another teacher who uses louder and louder commands cannot. The anecdotes in this book consistently reflect exceptionally good individual understanding of each child and of the living context in which the problem occurred. In their anecdotes most of the parents use a deft change in the environment to produce an effective solution.

BACKGROUND

This volume grew out of our 30 years' experience developing the first and only comprehensive statewide program for the *T*reatment and *E*ducation of *A*utistic and *C*ommunication *H*andicapped *CH*ildren (TEACCH). This university-based program was born in reaction to the misinformation and misunderstanding of autism taught according to Freudian doctrines and widely converted into social policy (Schopler, 1993). Autistic children were assumed to have withdrawn from the unconscious hostility and rejection of their parents, who were thought to be intellectually compulsive and emotionally cold. The treatment of choice was to remove the child from these parents, for placement in a psychiatric hospital or residential school to the exclusion of public school attendance. During the early years of TEACCH, our research and clinical experience helped to disprove these mistaken beliefs by showing that autism was produced by various biological causes and not by social withdrawal from unfavorable parenting attitudes. Parents were not the cause of the disorder; rather they were an essential part of the rehabilitation. They were necessary and effective collaborators with professionals in defining and carrying out the individual treatment process. We learned early on that children could best be helped through their parents in the public schools and in their own communities, regardless of whether they lived in the city or the country (Schopler & Reichler, 1971).

PARENT–PROFESSIONAL COLLABORATION

In developing the nation's first and only comprehensive statewide program for the treatment and education of autistic and similar people (Mesibov, in press; Schopler, 1994; Schopler, Mesibov, Shigley & Bashford, 1984), we soon learned that for professionals, the parents' perspective was the single most important view to shape and inform both our treatment program and our research. It meant an equal working relationship in which our staff learned from and used the parents' unique experiences with their own child, and in which, as professionals, we offered the parents our knowledge of the field and our experience with many children. Parents collaborated with us in defining our program priorities. Together we focused on a public school program, respite care, summer camp, group homes, supported employment, preschool programs, and others.

A holistic or parents' perspective informed our multidisciplinary training in the generalist model. This meant that we expected our trainees, whether social workers, educators, psychologists, speech pathologists, psychiatrists, or others, to have a working knowledge of all the problems raised by autism, not just the special angles they studied in their professional schools. From the parents' perspective, we learned some important lessons from the children's autism, best summarized in six operating principles in addition to the importance of parent–professional collaboration. Whereas these have been conceptualized by professionals, parents and their anecdotes reflect them intuitively.

1. *Adaptation.* We found that autism usually involves a lifelong struggle. We do not subscribe to the proposal advocated by some highly regarded researchers and funding agencies, that if we are not looking for a cure, we are not doing anything. Instead, we believe our mission is to improve each individual's adaptation to the world he or she lives in right now. This is done in at least two ways: first, by improving all skills for living with the best available educational techniques; second, by accommodating the environment to any impeding deficit. Both of these processes are needed to improve adaptation.

2. *Assessment.* Careful evaluation of each individual involves both formal assessment (the best and most appropriate tests available) and informal assessment (the best and most thoughtful observations possible) by teachers, parents, and all others in regular contact with the child. In other words, the best understanding of each individual's learning or behavior problems and strengths is needed to identify the best individualized treatment

available. This observation process is illustrated in most of the anecdotes in subsequent chapters.

3. *Structured teaching.* The large majority of our autistic population has some special learning problems and strengths. They have trouble organizing themselves, difficulty in processing auditory information, and memory lapses, especially for things outside their special interests. On the other hand, they have special memory skills, specific interests, and strengths in processing visual information. These skills can be used effectively for teaching independence and learning. Not only can visual structures promote learning and independence, they also facilitate linkage between home, school, and the workplace (Mesibov, Schopler, & Hearsey, 1994). Equally important, structured teaching prevents behavior problems, many of which are rooted in nonfunctional communication and frustration. The few behavior problems unresponsive to structured teaching are discussed below. Many of the anecdotes in this manual are based on the structured teaching principle. Recognition of the frequent occurrence of visual strengths in autism came from the experience of professionals (Schopler, Mesibov, & Hearsey, 1995).

4. *Priority to skill enhancement.* The most effective teaching approach is to use and enhance existing skills and recognize with acceptance the shortcomings to be improved. This approach is important not only for teaching children and adults, but also for parents, staff, and other professionals.

5. *Theories of behavior and cognition.* The most useful educational intervention and behavior management is based on behavior and cognitive theory. Unlike psychoanalytic and similar theories, these can be tested and checked with empirical research and accountability data. Cognitive theory takes into account differences according to developmental levels. For example, when teaching spontaneous communication (Watson, Lord, Schaffer & Schopler, 1989), we build on the child's existing level of communication, be it bodily movement or use of objects, pictures, or words. We analyze the communicative

intent, be it a request, a bid for attention, rejection, giving or seeking information. We also analyze the semantics involved and consider the context in which the communication takes place. New words are then taught in the familiar context of home or the classroom, while established words are taught in new contexts like the play yard or grandmother's house.

On the other hand, behavior theory is used and illustrated by the iceberg metaphor discussed later in this chapter. It is also applied with great frequency by parents and teachers in the anecdotes making up the body of this manual.

6. *Generalist model.* Professionals from any discipline interested in working with this population are trained as generalists. This means we expect them to have a working ability to deal with the whole range of problems raised by autism, regardless of their specialty training. This enables them to take responsibility for the whole child and refer to specialists when appropriate. This model also teaches the parents' perspective, for parents are expected to function as generalists for their own child, whether or not he or she has special needs.

SELECTION OF TREATMENT TECHNIQUES

For a parent first encountering the diagnosis of autism, the possible choices of available treatment techniques can present costly and overwhelming choices. Many such therapies and treatment concepts have appeared in the public press and professional journals during the past decades. Table 1–1 presents over two dozen techniques, but these are not all-inclusive.

Rimland (1994) refers to over 100 treatment techniques, including about 30 drugs. These techniques are frequently heralded with great excitement by parents convinced that they have witnessed the miraculous improvement they have been searching for, or by professionals hoping for the fame and rewards of finding a cure. Unfortunately, the road to scientific progress is fraught with false hopes. Too often these techniques are only the product of successful marketing and media hype. The data do not support the technique's intended usefulness and often result in a short-lived fad. Some of these techniques are promoted

Table 1–1. Specific Therapies with Autism

Aversive	Mainstreaming
Auditory training	Megavitamin
Dance	Music
Deinstitutionalization	Patterning
Developmental	Pharmacotherapy
Dolphin	Phenothiazine
Electroconvulsive	Physical
Facilitated communication	Play
Feingold diet	Pony
Fenfluramine	Psychogenesis
Holding	Sensory integration
Intensive behavior	Signing
Interactive	Speech
Logo	

as ideologies to be converted to social policies. These run the risk of producing unexpected negative consequences. Examples include psychoanalytic theory and facilitated communication, discussed in the following sections.

This discussion of treatment choice would be out of place if we knew how to prevent or cure autism. But because this is not yet the case, different forms for fostering improvement must still be implemented by each family struggling with the challenges of autism. The Autism Society of America has recognized this state of affairs by giving parental choice priority in their mission statement. These choices depend on the lifestyle of the family, where they live, and what professional resources are available to them.

Psychoanalytic Theory

We have already referred to the misunderstanding and suffering produced by the use of psychoanalytic theory for explaining autism. These children were usually excluded from public schools and were separated from their parents with residential placement as the therapy of choice. This often had the effect of demoralizing parents unnecessarily while preventing children from participating in community life. It is now widely recognized that this treatment was based on a misunderstanding of autism; it was erroneously classified as an emotional problem rather than one based on disordered neurobiologic processes, as shown by a vast body of empirical research (Schopler & Mesibov, 1987). Nevertheless, there are several European countries in which disproven psychoanalytic practices for treating autism are still dominant. For example, only about a decade ago in France, no other treatment options were available. It is interesting to note that even under such unfavorable circumstances, several families believed that their child had made important progress under psychoanalytic treatment. This shows that even with an erroneous theory that has had disastrous consequences as social policy, some individuals can improve when no other options are available. Facilitated communication is another technique with a potential for misunderstanding and mischief on a scale similar to psychoanalysis.

Facilitated Communication

Facilitated communication (FC) was developed over a decade ago in Australia by Rosemary Crossley, a speech therapist who worked with a few clients with cerebral palsy who were thought to be mentally retarded. A therapist or "facilitator" steadied the client's hand or arm while the client spelled out the message to be communicated. This process produced some remarkably sophisticated messages, along with claims of unexpected high intellectual function, by clients thought by some to be severely retarded. An Australian review panel found no validation of high intellectual functioning for individuals diagnosed with either cerebral palsy or autism. Moreover, the panel reported a strong suspicion that "facilitated communication" originated with the facilitator and not with the client. In Australia, as a result of research and independent review, FC was no longer attributed with unusual therapeutic powers, but was again regarded as just one of several augmented communication techniques. At the same time, an American special educator, Douglas Biklen (1991), returned from Australia proclaiming FC as a new breakthrough for understanding and treating autism. He and his followers proclaimed that more than 90% of autistic children had broken through their communication barriers. However, study after study showed that communication originated with the facilitator, and when the facilitator was kept from knowing the question, no significant communication usually took place (Green & Shane, 1994). When FC advocates were confronted with such research evidence, they blithely dismissed the empirical research because they claimed it violated the trust and faith in the relationship that was supposedly the foundation of FC success.

Perhaps it is not surprising that despite these serious criticisms, a number of parents witnessing their offspring expressing love for the first time were enthusiastic and grateful for FC regardless of where the message originated. Unfortunately, when a technique is marketed and promoted beyond supporting research evidence, many unexpected and costly side effects can develop. Because FC advocates deny the usefulness of empirical research, they do not determine the most suitable augmented communication technique for a particular child. Facilitators have been assigned to mute children capable of typing on their own and to children with good verbal skills who need help building a spoken vocabulary, not in guided typing. Individuals like these are deprived of the optimum individualized communication techniques, including choice among computers, picture cards, coding systems, symbol pointers, and other such augmented communication techniques.

Another perhaps more destructive side effect of the FC overzealousness is the growing number of court cases, both here and in Europe, initiated against parents or caretakers, with allegations of sexual abuse based only on FC evidence. Although FC evidence has invariably been thrown out of court, the families involved have had their lives irreversibly disrupted.

Facilitated communication is similar to psychoanalysis in that both are based on unproven theories and their advocates deny the relevance of empirical research. Both claim that beneath emotional or social inhibitions a nonhandicapped individual awaits release. Both theories have been used to blame parents or caretakers with either unconscious and/or sexual child abuse. Yet both therapies have convinced some parents and professionals that they have witnessed an effective course of treatment with a particular child.

It is not within the scope of this manual to critique every treatment technique listed in Table 1–1; however, we can underscore some points they all have in common.

1. *Good idea.* Both concepts or techniques seemed like a reasonably good idea to the initiator and colleagues. Sometimes the techniques have been known to correct another problem, as in FC for cerebral palsy, or to add a corrective element with an additional technique. But regardless of the source, the initiator was convinced it was worthwhile to apply this technique to the entire autistic population.

2. *Anecdotal cure.* There are usually one or a few cases that appear to show striking improvement, sometimes referred to as a cure. But because it was a single case anecdote, the specific reasons for the improvement are far from clear. It could have been due to any number of factors, including a spontaneous fluctuation of behavior. Such pilot success stories are often picked up by the news-hungry media, popular magazines, and professional journals. The resulting excitement promotes premature widespread use of the technique and confusion between pilot studies and demonstrated effectiveness.

3. *Limited effectiveness.* Excessive media attention to pilot research can inflate the number of researchers flocking for available funds to replicate the advertised miracle. These replications are often based on unlikely hypotheses, without adequate theoretical bases, but promoted mainly by hype and hope. Regardless of how the techniques are repeated, not a single treatment technique has been effective with all or even most autistic children.

4. *Costs and side effects.* Continued use has shown that each technique has costs and negative side effects, not considered or predicted by the initiators in the flush of the pilot study drama.

5. *Source of ineffectiveness.* The kinds of commonly occurring treatment ineffectiveness are:

    a. *When the theory is widely accepted, but empirical research is not available or not sought by the initiators.* This was clearly the case with psychoanalysis and facilitated communication.

b. *When the available empirical evidence does not adequately support claims of effectiveness.* For example, with certain diets and with auditory training, effectiveness may not be measured until 9 months later. In the case of diets, the change could be due to other dietary components. For example, to make a diet work, often the entire family has to use more carefully structured eating habits. With auditory training, often the special sound sensitivities are not modified, but some behaviors improve for many possible reasons, including more structured listening sessions.

c. *When the treatment procedure becomes a political ideology imposed on all whether they like it or not.* For example, total inclusion, sometimes referred to as required classroom integration, is desirable for some individuals but quite negative for others. Deinstitutionalization helped to close many snakepitlike institutions, but then produced increasing numbers of street people that the ideologists did not represent. In short, when treatment procedures are turned into political ideologies, they may be effective for some individuals but deny the special needs of others.

Most of the techniques listed in Table 1–1 do not have the costly and negative side effects of psychoanalytic theory and FC. In the absence of a cure or demonstrated treatment for all autistic children, parents should select those specific techniques most appropriate for their child, depending on the family's location, the resources available, and the individual needs of their child. They can make their selection by reading, by consulting with professionals in their community, or by contacting a professional consultant to one of the parents' groups listed in Chapter 9. Regardless of what treatment approach a particular family adopts, they will be dealing with their own unique behavior problems and challenges. Although most of the solutions presented in this manual were submitted by only one family, a few were presented more often. In addition, some anecdotes fit equally well under more than one chapter, and may be cross-referenced. Neither we nor the informing families claim any one to be the only solution. However, we hope they will give you both ideas and inspiration for solving some of the special problems autism has brought to your attention.

GUIDE TO CHAPTERS

Historically, in our three decade's experience with Division TEACCH, the most consistent correction and prevention of behavior problems have resulted from the treatment concepts used in our community-based program described above, with special emphasis on the use of visual structures adapted for use at home, at school, and in the workplace. But even under these conditions, some behavior problems occur at times. These are best understood in the form of the iceberg metaphor shown in Figure 1–1. This iceberg represents problems of aggression. Above the water line are specific aggressive behaviors like pushing, hitting, spitting, throwing, and so on. Under the water line, out of sight, are various autism deficits or possible trigger mechanisms for the aggressive behavior. These could include poor social judgment, unawareness of feelings of self or others, sensory misperception, frustration over communication problems, and others. By careful observation of the circumstances and conditions under which the behavior occurred both in the past and in the present, we can usually figure out the most likely explanation. For example, 5-year-old Bill was slapping at his teacher and others in a repetitive manner. His teacher thought perhaps he was slapping because he did not have any other communication signal for gaining her attention. Since he had no words, she taught him to raise a picture of the teacher when he wanted her to come. As he learned to use the picture, the slapping decreased in frequency and stopped 3 weeks later. The communication deficit explanation was clearly on target. If the slapping had not decreased, a different explanation would have to be found, leading to a different intervention.

The anecdotes making up the body of Chapters 2–8 contain the same kind of analysis just reviewed for the iceberg metaphor for aggression. Each anecdote is followed by a discussion written by the member of our TEACCH staff who assembled the anecdotes in that chapter. It includes our analysis of the behavior, what may have

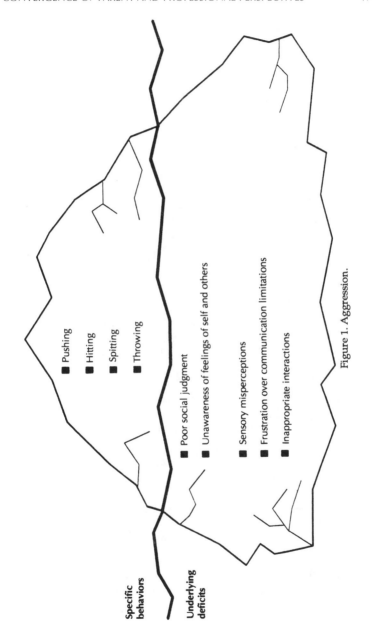

Specific behaviors

- Pushing
- Hitting
- Spitting
- Throwing

Underlying deficits

- Poor social judgment
- Unawareness of feelings of self and others
- Sensory misperceptions
- Frustration over communication limitations
- Inappropriate interactions

Figure 1. Aggression.

triggered it, and what had been done to prevent or change the behavior. References to behavioral research are sometimes cited. These often show that parents intuitively discover approaches similar to those found by professional research. The reference sections also offer additional reading, should you want to know more about a particular topic.

In many instances, the anecdotal story could have been listed under more than one of the chapter headings. Likewise, more than one behavior intervention could have been used. If our grouping seems arbitrary, the intent was to make it easier for the reader to locate the topic of interest. Mostly we are trying to emphasize the importance of understanding your child and his or her behavior through thoughtful observation. We also provide examples of how this can reduce or prevent behavior problems with solutions that fit your own style of living.

Each chapter has a copy of the iceberg on the first page of the chapter. It identifies the behaviors and the page numbers of the anecdote in which the behavior appears, with the explanatory deficits under the waterline. This arrangement serves as a table of contents for that chapter.

Chapter 8 is intended as a guide for behavior management in situations not responsive to the two kinds of situations discussed so far. To review, the first is the prevention of behavior problems through using visual structures and the applicable concepts discussed above. But even when all preventive structures have been put in operation, a certain number of behavior problems are likely to occur, as they do with children without special needs. The majority of those problems can be handled according to the anecdotal examples supplied by parents, using the kind of thinking represented by the iceberg metaphor.

For the few behavior problems that are not responsive to these two approaches, the more traditional behavior modification procedures are outlined in Chapter 8. Included here are different systems of reward tokens, and procedures like differential reinforcement, extinction, time out, and social reinforcement.

In Chapter 9, we summarize some of the reasons and ways for organizing community support. Alice Wertheimer offers a succinct summary of how she first discovered the importance of support from parents with similar concerns. She reviews how parents organized their group in Chapel Hill, North Carolina, including their Resource Guide for locating autism-sensitive restaurants, dentists, and other professionals. This is followed by a listing of both state and national societies, including the Professional Panel of Advisors for the Autism Society of America and a list of related books and publications.

In summary, we have compiled anecdotes of home-grown coping successes with various problems posed by the autism syndrome. We teach the process by which parents arrived at these problem solutions, and we relate these to some of the behavioral research. We then expand the support from personal experience to formal local units, state societies, and national organizations. The material represents a process in motion, one that may inspire members of the autism community to find new experiences that will prove helpful in the future.

REFERENCES

American Psychiatric Association. 1994. *Diagnostic and Statistical Manual of Mental Disorders* (4th ed.). Washington, DC: Author.

Biklen, D. (1991). Communication unbound: Autism and praxis. *Harvard Educational Review, 60,* 291–314.

Green, G., & Shane, H. C. (1994). Science, reason, and Facilitated Communication. *Journal of the Association for Persons with Severe Handicaps, 19,* 151–172.

Kanner, L. (1943). Autistic disturbances of affective contact. *Nervous Child, 2,* 217–250.

Mesibov, G. B. (in press). Division TEACCH: A collaborative model program for service delivery training, and research for people with autism and related communication handicaps. In M. C. Roberts (Ed.), *Model Programs in service delivery in child and family mental health.* New York: Plenum Press.

Mesibov, G. B., Schopler, E., & Hearsey, K. A. (1994). Structured teaching. In E. Schopler & G. B. Mesibov (Eds.), *Behavioral issues in autism* (pp. 195–210). New York: Plenum Press.

Rimland, B. (1994). Facilitated communication: What's going on? *Autism Research Review, 6,* 4, 2.

Schopler, E. (1993). Anatomy of a negative role model. In G. Brannigan & M. Merrens (Eds.), *The undaunted psychologist* (pp. 173–186). New York: McGraw-Hill.

Schopler, E. (1994). A statewide program for the treatment and education of autistic and related communication handicapped children (TEACCH). *Child and Adolescent Psychiatric Clinics of North America 3(1),* 91–103.

Schopler, E., & Mesibov, G. B. (1987). *Neurological issues in autism.* New York: Plenum Press.

Schopler, E., Mesibov, G. B., & Hearsey, K. (1995). Structured teaching in the TEACCH system. In E. Schopler & G. B. Mesibov (Eds.), *Learning and cognition in autism* (pp. 243–268). New York: Plenum Press.

Schopler, E., Mesibov, G. B., Shigley, R. H., & Bashford, A. (1984). Helping autistic children through their parents: The TEACCH method. In E. Schopler & G. B. Mesibov (Eds.), *The effects of autism on the family* (pp. 65–81). New York: Plenum Press.

Schopler, E., & Reichler, R. J. (1971). Parents as cotherapists. *Journal of Autism and Childhood Schizophrenia, 1,* 87, 102.

Schopler, E., & Reichler, R. J. (1972). Parents as cotherapists. In S. Chess & A. Thomas (Eds.), *Annual progress in child psychiatry and child development* (pp. 679–697). New York: Brunner/Mazel.

Watson, L., Lord, C., Schaffer, B., & Schopler, E. (1989). *Teaching spontaneous communication to autistic and developmentally handicapped children.* Austin, TX: Pro-Ed.

2

Repetitive Behaviors and Special Interests

Runs out of church   24   Touches compulsively   25   Plays
with doors   26   Unties shoes   27   Tidies compulsively   28
Kisses, fondles feet   29   Hates bedsheets changed   29
Paces off rooms   30   Overeats and sits   31   Mouths
shirt   32   Licks hands   32   Plays in water   33   Drops
objects into floor vents   34   Flushes soap down toilet   34
Flaps arms, twirls, spins   35   Taps plates, glasses,
bowls   37   Upset, change of familiar object   37   Upset over
punctuality   38   Runs to swimming pool   39   Repeats
words   39   Questions constantly   40

**Problem
Behaviors**

Poor impulse control   25   Driven by special interests   29
Communication problems   25   Can't differentiate   27
Lacks awareness of social rules of standards   29   Dislikes
change   37   Preoccupation with numbers   31   Repetitive
physical movements   30   Needs sensory stimulation with
tongue and skin   32   Obsession with water   33
Preoccupation with visual movement   34   Fluttering,
moving   35   Preoccupation with time   38   Need for
rituals   39

**Underlying
Deficits**

R epetitive behaviors and special interests are defining features of autism described not only in Kanner's original paper (1943), but also in each of the revised versions of the *Diagnostic and Statistical Manual* of the American Psychiatric Association (1994). People with autism and others who engage in repetitive behavior seem driven or under pressure to carry out the activity in a certain way. When such routines are interfered with, the person usually becomes anxious and unhappy, which often results in a wide range of behavior problems.

These behaviors and special interests can take many different forms and can vary with developmental function. At an early developmental level, stereotyped behaviors can be in the form of hand flapping, finger twisting, twirling, and spinning of objects. They involve sensory peculiarities like excessive licking, smelling, or making odd sounds.

At another level of development, preoccupations may include lining up objects, flicking light switches, or showing attachment to an object like a string, a nail, rubber tubing, or a toy. Interest may be expressed in part of a toy, such as a wheel, without concern for the whole object.

At a high level of developmental function, obsessive interests may relate to phone schedules, birth dates, weather reports, and commercials. They can involve more complex interests like plumbing diagrams, maps, or stories by Charles Dickens. For many people, changes in the route to school, in customary arrangements of furniture, or in school activities may cause extreme distress. All these behaviors are only examples of the tip of the iceberg discussed in Chapter 1 and are not an all-inclusive list. They are easy to recognize, but to understand some of the underlying mechanisms, it is important to know the individual child.

Repetitive behaviors may show up when a child is bored or frustrated, especially from social and communication problems typical of autism and similar developmental disorders. Some research data suggest a possible biochemical basis for such repetitive preoccupations (Breese, Mueller, & Schroeder, 1987).

Both parents and professionals have had difficulty understanding and managing repetitive behaviors. Too often attempts are made to eliminate these behaviors with standard behavior management techniques, rather than trying to understand the trigger mechanisms and what the behaviors can mean for the person. For this category of behavior, it is worthwhile to keep in mind that repetition and special interests not only have the potential for creating special behavior problems, but also can produce special skills, talents, and work habits that can be shaped into productive social and vocational contributions. In our experience, parents are often the first to find positive aspects of the child's special interest. This may take the form of working out a compromise between the child's special interest on the one hand, and the social requirements on the other. It may also set the stage for learning new skills applicable to socially useful activities. This chapter offers examples of sensitive and thoughtful responses by parents.

COMPULSIVE AND RITUALISTIC ROUTINES

Compulsive and ritualistic behaviors are those that the person appears compelled to perform in an exact way. Frequently, the child seems driven to carry them out and becomes upset if prevented from doing so. This creates great difficulties and may disrupt activities or interfere with household routines. For example, one autistic child felt compelled to close every door behind him and to turn off lights each time he left a room, even if other people were using the room. Compulsive and ritualistic behaviors can be embarrassing to parents in public and may cause family members to limit their involvement in community activities. Audrey, for example, insisted on going out the same door she entered at church, thereby threatening her family's church attendance. The father wrote the following:

> I missed going to church regularly, but it was hard to go with Audrey, my 11-year-old daughter. In the middle of the service, she would run down

the center aisle and out of the church. Not only did this effectively disrupt the service, but it also demonstrated an unusual behavior of Audrey's: Audrey *must* leave by the same door she entered.

One day I figured out how to put this autistic behavior to work for me. I realized that if Audrey left the church the back way, she would disturb no one. And the way to get her to leave the back way was to *enter* the back way. So now Audrey and I enter the church through the parking lot door and sit in the rear of the sanctuary, directly in front of the back door. If she jumps up to leave in the middle of the service, she runs out the back door without disturbing anyone. Now I attend church as often as I want.

Audrey feels a need to leave places by the same door that she enters. Although this may not create a problem at home, it is clearly a problem in public places such as church. Instead of trying to eliminate this behavior at church, Audrey's father accepted it and changed his own behavior in order to accommodate Audrey. By entering through the rear door, Audrey could maintain her ritual of leaving through the door she entered without disrupting the church service.

Because Audrey was able to wait outside safely, this solution was adequate. It was also compatible with Audrey's short attention span, which made an hour-long church service unbearably long for her. Her father did not punish the offending behavior, but recognized it as a nonverbal signal that the service had exceeded Audrey's tolerance level. For a younger child or one who cannot leave the church safely alone, the parent might have to look for an acceptable church school placement, shorten his own church stay, work on "breaking" the exit ritual, or bring along some toys or other materials for the child when she becomes restless.

This anecdote refers to a specific behavior that affected the parents' ability to attend church. Some compulsive behaviors, illustrated by the following example, are of a more general nature and interfere with the family's ability to go to a variety of public places.

From the time he could walk, Jasper, age 5, was compelled to touch or operate every switch, knob, or button that he saw. Once during a visit to a public aquarium, he turned off the lights to an entire floor, leaving everyone in darkness. In another instance, he shut down the escalator in a major department store. Attempts to discipline him by spanking, withholding treats, and placing him in "time out" all failed. Then at age 7, an observant school teacher noticed that his switch touching was not rebellious naughtiness to be punished, but instead was perhaps a lack of understanding of appropriate time and place. She assigned him the sole responsibility of turning the classroom light and the tape recorder on and off at specified times. This practice was carried on at home. As Jasper learned proper time and place, he was able to walk by switches without touching them.

Jasper's compulsion to turn switches on and off drastically interfered with his family's trips to public places. After attempts to eliminate the behavior with punishment failed, his teacher decided to structure the behavior by allowing Jasper to turn switches on and off at certain appropriate times. As he learned to take responsibility for turning the lights and the tape recorder on and off, she provided him with frequent opportunities to carry out his repetitive interest appropriately. By substituting compulsive switching with useful switching, she was able to replace an autistic symptom with a productive use of his special interests.

A similar behavior that several parents reported was the tendency of children to open or close doors. A parent of a young child described her means of managing this behavior:

> My son Tommy, who is 5, is obsessed with doors. He feels a need to close every door behind him as he leaves a room and will play with doors for hours, opening and closing them. We decided to teach him more appropriate behavior by using a toy garage set. For a while, we let him play "open door/shut door, open/shut." Then we introduced other toys and taught him to open the door, put the car in, and shut the door only when the car was inside. Eventually, we found that he became comfortable with leaving the doors open and playing with the car and other toys.

Tommy's preoccupation with doors was an annoyance to his family and also prevented him from being involved in more appropriate play activities. His parents gave him a set of toys that enabled him to play with doors without using actual doors. These parents noticed that their son's disruptive preoccupation with doors was related to his inability to engage in symbolic play, a common problem with such children. With toys such as cars, they showed him a variety of interesting activities for opening and closing doors. The play helped Tommy to broaden his activities without giving up his special interests in doors. By introducing other toys such as cars, they stimulated his interest in other toys and allowed him to ignore open doors comfortably.

Some ritualistic activities may develop from the child's lack of understanding of how to use objects properly. Here a parent describes her son's compulsive behavior and how she became aware of what was causing it:

> When Jack was 7 years old, he developed an annoying habit of constantly untying shoes, both his own and others'. Professionals suggested a behavior modification approach that included taking his own shoes away from him when he persisted in untying them. He did not like to go shoeless, so it was felt this would be a good punishment. This didn't work, however. He continued to go after shoelaces he saw on other people. Then one morning, each time I completed the first tying motion, he pulled his foot away to see what I had done. Suddenly I realized that untying shoes was not a "behavior problem," but his way of showing us that he wanted to learn to tie shoes! Every time he untied shoes, he would then have the opportunity to watch them being tied. He's left-handed and so is his older brother, so we had a competent teacher. In less than half a dozen sessions, he learned to tie his own shoes and the "behavior problem" stopped.

As his mother pointed out, Jack's seemingly annoying behavior was caused by his inability to tie his shoes, his desire to learn how, and his inability to tell anyone what he wanted. Once his mother realized what the underlying problem was, her solution was straightforward: teach Jack how to tie his own shoes. She was also perceptive enough to enlist Jack's left-handed brother as the instructor. This anecdote points out the importance of trying to understand the child's unusual communication efforts. This is another example of converting preoccupation to constructive behavior. His mother looked for a reason for the behavior rather than just trying to eliminate it. Not all repetitive behaviors have such a clear purpose, but parents can often tune in to the messages their children are sending.

Another typical compulsive behavior that parents report is the tendency to keep rooms neat by putting everything away. In some children, this behavior is so extreme that the child tries to put away almost every object in the house—even those that are meant to be left out.

Billy likes everything to be kept neat in our house. He likes to put things away, although not always where they belong. We have an antique chair that has knobs on the arms. He took one off and put it away so that we couldn't find it. I realized that I had to motivate him to find it. I got a bottle of glue, which he likes, and put it by the chair. I said, "If only we could find the knob, we could glue it on." Billy went out of the room and immediately came back with the "lost" knob.

Clearly, Billy's habit of putting everything away became a bit too much. Since Billy did not understand the difference between objects like knobs and chairs that are meant to be left out and toys that need to be put away, his mother used an external motivator to encourage him to find the knob. The glue not only was a favorite object of his, but was useful in solving the problem of replacing the knob on the chair.

Another mother described her son as their "Felix" (the superneat partner in the movie *The Odd Couple*):

Roger is our Felix. Sometimes he drives us crazy putting everything away. I decided that the problem wasn't that he was neat, but that he was too neat at the wrong times (putting things away while we were still using them). I decided to think of his neatness as a strength and put him in charge of the kids' Saturday morning family room cleanup. Now nobody quits until every toy and scrap of paper is picked up and the room is spotless. The other kids call him "the boss" (as in, "Watch out. If you stick that under the cushion, the boss will get you!"). They seem relieved to realize there are some things he does better than they do. Who knows, his teenage brother may even "catch" a little of his neatness.

In this case, Roger's mother analyzed her child's behavior to discover what aspect of it was negative and what aspect was positive. By structuring an activity where his neatness was appropriate, Roger was able to accomplish something important for the family and obtain some appreciation from them.

UNUSUAL OR RESTRICTED INTERESTS

Another type of ritualistic behavior is the development of unusual interests. One way that these interests are shown is in the child's attachment to a special object. Some children will carry these objects around and refuse to part with them. Other children may show an extreme reaction each time they come into contact with a particular object. These attachments may look bizarre and get the child into difficulty. One parent writes of his son's unusual interest:

> Our son Jerry, 18, was on a trial basis in a supported employment position where he was causing difficulties because of his particular interest in feet. He loved to touch, kiss, and fondle feet. His need to pursue this interest varied from one time to another and was unpredictable. When he dove on some unsuspecting woman, longing only to be near her feet, the victim was usually quite upset.
>
> Because this behavior had been a long-standing one, we accepted the idea that Jerry was unlikely to lose interest in feet and shoes. Therefore, we worked out a compromise. He was told that he could ask the objects of his passion if he could polish their shoes. He was set up with a shoe-shining station including all the necessary equipment. Now he knows that he doesn't have to attack someone's feet and shoes to have some quick contact before he is stopped. He knows that instead he can choose one or two people each day and offer to shine their shoes during the lunch hour. While he has the shoes, he is welcome to touch them at the shoe-shine station but not on a person.

This young man's unusual interest in feet had a high potential for social misunderstanding. Again his parents and supportful employment staff hit on a resourceful solution for turning the problem into a constructive activity. They taught Jerry how to shine shoes and gave him rules that would help manage the behavior: he was allowed to choose one or two people per day, and shoes could be touched only at the shoe-shining station during his lunch hour. His motivation to touch shoes was so high that he complied with the rules. His foot "fetish" became a productive shoe-shining routine.

Another parent describes an attachment her daughter had to a special object:

> Our 10-year-old daughter, Beth, had a fit every time I took her favorite sheets off her bed to put clean ones on. Every week we went through a battle when I tried to change her sheets. Finally, I discovered that if I had her help me take the favorite sheets off and put the clean ones on, the sheets could be changed without a fight. We now have the routine of changing the sheets every Saturday morning, and there have been no further arguments.

This mother's solution both overcame Beth's special attachment to her favorite sheets and promoted her self-help skills. Once Beth felt that she was part of the activity of changing the sheets, her resistance to removing them decreased and clean sheets could be put on the bed. Her mother capitalized on Beth's love of routines to include her in the sheet changing. Once changing sheets became part of her routine, it also helped Beth understand where the sheets went when they were taken off and helped her anticipate their eventual return.

In middle childhood or adolescence, some people with autism develop new, unusual preoccupations. These special interests take up a great deal of their time and can prevent involvement in other activities. Many of these preoccupations pertain to accumulating factual information, such as memorizing maps, studying bus schedules, or showing a fascination with dates. A group home house parent described an autistic adult who demonstrated this type of behavior:

> Steven, age 21, had the ritualistic behavior of pacing throughout houses he visited. His behavior was socially difficult because he would walk continuously throughout the entire house. Before an annual Christmas party, the hostess took Steven on a tour of the house so that he was able to see the house in a socially acceptable way. She told Steven which rooms he could go into and which rooms were off limits, saying "Don't go in if the door is shut." The hostess then set up coat storage in the room farthest away from the entrance on the upper floor. Steven was given the job of putting away the guests' coats. Each time the doorbell rang, Steven took the guests' coats and went up the stairs and through the house to the back bedroom. He also retrieved coats for guests at the end of the party. This allowed Steven to tour the house in a socially acceptable way.

The hostess came up with the thoughtful solution of assigning Steven the role of coat-taker during the party. This allowed him to combine his socially inappropriate preoccupation with "pacing off" floor plans with socially useful trips from room to room helping with coats. This also forced him to interact with guests while taking their coats, and it provided a courtesy that the guests appreciated. Steven's smile showed how much he enjoyed "pacing off" the house and made him a welcoming host when he took guests' coats at the door.

Another mother reported how she used her son's unusual preoccupations to help him lose weight:

Mickey is an overweight 26-year-old man who has been a TV addict for many years. He refused to go on a diet or exercise in order to lose weight. He has always been fascinated by numbers, particularly counting and sports, so I decided to take advantage of both interests. I encouraged Mickey to watch TV programs that were about exercising, such as the "Richard Simmons Show." I then bought him a jogging suit and shoes. We measured the distance between the mailbox and house steps and multiplied this so that Mickey knew how many laps equaled 1 mile. Every day he would watch an exercise show and then run 1 mile by counting his laps. Next, I got him to agree to a diet by giving him a calorie guide book. He was fascinated with all the numbers in the book, and agreed to count his daily calories without going over a set limit. Through the combination of exercise and diet, Mickey was able to lose weight.

This anecdote provides a dramatic example of how to use an unusual preoccupation with numbers and routines as a motivation for doing something that otherwise would hold no interest. Mickey did not exercise or diet, because the social and health consequences of being overweight were not important to him. However, his fascination with numbers and sports was so strong that he agreed to count laps for jogging and calories for dieting. The combination of exercise and diet helped him to lose weight and improve his physical fitness. The mother provided a jogging suit at a fixed time each day so that her son had a clear signal as to when his jogging back and forth was appropriate.

STEREOTYPED BEHAVIOR

Stereotyped behaviors, sometimes called autistic behaviors, include odd mannerisms and unusual sensory interests. Odd mannerisms include hand flapping, finger flicking, tics, or toe walking. Some children may display a pronounced interest in only a part of an object, such as endlessly spinning a wheel on a toy truck. These are sometimes referred to as "self-stimulatory" behaviors because they seem to have no purpose other than self-stimulation. Besides their lack of obvious purpose, these behaviors look bizarre and can interfere with more useful behaviors.

It is usually well worth the effort to convert these behaviors into more useful ones. When unable to do that, some parents have tried to eliminate the behavior. This most often requires creativity and has led to a variety of techniques developed by parents and professionals.

> At the age of 6, Frank would always put his shirt in his mouth. The shirts occupied most of his attention and eventually would be ruined. We tried a variety of things to stop him, including putting Tabasco sauce on his shirts. None of these things worked. One day I had him wear a wool sweater over his shirt and noticed how distasteful the wool seemed to him when he mouthed it. Then we had him start wearing wool sweaters regularly. He couldn't stand the taste of wool, so he didn't put the sweaters in his mouth. Fortunately, the habit was broken before the warm weather set in!

Frank had the habit of putting his shirts in his mouth for no apparent reason. Because his parents could find no constructive use for this habit, they tried to eliminate it. However, even the strong deterrent, Tabasco sauce, did not eliminate the behavior. Having him wear wool sweaters was successful because he did not like the taste or the texture of the wool in his mouth. Some researchers have developed another approach, called overcorrection, to eliminate mouthing of objects (Foxx & Azrin, 1973). With this technique, the child overcorrects the undesirable behavior. For example, a child who liked to mouth objects had to rinse his mouth with mouthwash five times after each mouthing of an object.

Another form of stereotyped behavior is licking objects or one's hands. Some researchers have suggested that children do this when they lack the skills for using objects appropriately, and they settle for the sensory feedback from licking instead. In other words, hands may be stimulating to a child who has very few play skills. One study suggested a procedure called sensory extinction, in which the sensory feedback that the child would receive was blocked or reduced (Aiken & Salzberg, 1984). Here a parent describes how she accomplished this:

> Our 11-year-old daughter, Carrie, was constantly licking her hands. We decided to make her wear plastic gloves. When she had plastic gloves on, she didn't lick her hands. We also found that after she took the gloves

off, her hands tasted like the gloves, which prevented her from licking her hands for several more hours.

Mouthing one's hands is more acceptable for an infant than for an 11-year-old girl. The plastic gloves kept her from getting the skin and tongue stimulation that she enjoyed. Without this pleasurable sensation, she stopped licking her hands. One researcher (Richmond, 1983) reduced excessive hand mouthing by three profoundly retarded adolescent girls. When he saw them start mouthing, he simply told them "No! Hands down!" and pushed their hands down. After several weeks, this simple procedure succeeded in reducing their hand mouthing.

Some people with autism like to use objects in nonfunctional ways. For example, they may spin or twirl toys or compulsively line up objects. Water play is another example of such obsessive behavior.

Timmy is 8 years old and has been intrigued by water for as long as I can remember. He will play in it all day if we allow him to and will find it in the toilet or wherever he can. Punishing him doesn't seem to stop him. I decided to go along with him and try to make his interest in water play useful. I taught Timmy how to wash and rinse the dishes. This has become his chore, and he loves to do it. Now, Timmy washes the dishes every night after dinner.

Timmy, like most children, is fascinated by water. After many attempts to break this obsession, his mother turned it into something positive by teaching him how to wash dishes. This channeled his obsession into an appropriate outlet and taught him a useful family contribution—dishwashing. The basis of this successful solution was the mother's realization that Timmy was not trying to misbehave. Instead, she recognized an important clue to his learning. She found a way to channel that interest into a skill useful around the house.

Many stereotyped preoccupations are with visually interesting objects. Colorful spinning toys, such as tops or kaleidoscopes, are fun to look at and are often the favorite toys of young autistic children. A child who likes the sound of spinning objects on a table might like to play and hear music on a record player. This could replace the self-stimulatory behavior with a good leisure skill.

Two other common behavioral preoccupations that parents report are watching things fall and flushing things down the toilet. This is illustrated in the following anecdote:

> At age 9, Alice was constantly dropping things down the floor vents in our classroom. She loved looking through the vents and watching the hot air blow things as they fluttered down into the vent. This stuffed up the heating vents so that they didn't work. We put a box over one of the vents with an opening on top and "windows" on the sides of the box. This way Alice could put something in the hole in the top of the box and watch it fall fluttering in the air draft, but the objects wouldn't go down the vents. Alice earned the chance to use her "hot air box" by completing a gradually increasing number of classroom working sessions. Gradually, she lost interest in this activity and we were able to move the box away from the vent and switch to a regular play time for work completion.

Alice's interest in moving pieces might also be extended to learning to use a kaleidoscope. By observing closely and finding what kind of stimulation (visual, auditory, and so on) the child is seeking, it is sometimes possible to find a more appropriate (and controllable) source of this stimulation. Since this type of stimulation is then known to be a powerful reinforcer for that particular child, it can be used as a free-play activity and/or as a reinforcer for completing less desired activities.

> Last year, we went through a period when Jim (age 10) was flushing the soap down the toilet. It would spin around in the bowl and go down the drain . . . great excitement! The soap would go down, coating the trap and clogging the toilet. I tried every behavior modifying trick in the book, but none of them worked. Finally, someone said, "Why don't you buy Ivory; it floats?" Since it floats, Jim can't watch it go down the drain. This took away all the fun for him, and he has stopped flushing soap down the toilet.

Both Alice and Jim had repetitive behaviors that held their visual interest. Dropping things down heating vents and flushing soap down the toilet both interfered with good housekeeping efforts. Their parents and teachers became frustrated with clogged toilets and stuffed-up heating vents. In both cases, they did not assume that the children were being deliberately destructive. Instead they determined what part of the behavior was holding the child's interest. In one case, the teacher found a harmless way for the child to enjoy her fascination with blowing objects and used it as a reward for appropriate behavior. In the other case, the parent eliminated the "payoff" of watching the soap flush down the toilet. Once the visual excitement was decreased, the behavior soon stopped.

Hand flapping and finger flicking are commonly mentioned stereotyped behaviors. Parents report that their children will engage in these behaviors as a way of occupying themselves, although hand flapping may increase when the child is nervous or excited. These behaviors often interfere with other activities. Parents are also bothered by the strange appearance of hand movements. One solution suggested by researchers is overcorrection (Epstein, Doke, Satwaj, Sorrell, & Rimmer, 1974; Foxx & Azrin, 1973), which involves telling the child that the behavior is inappropriate and insisting on a repetitive, positive replacement activity using the same part of the body. The child might have to open and close his hand repeatedly or, more commonly, use his hands repeatedly in a useful activity.

Physical exercise such as jogging has also been used to decrease self-stimulatory behaviors (Kern, Koegel, & Dunlap, 1984). Some researchers believe that regular physical exercise improves children's alertness and helps them pay attention to appropriate tasks without being distracted by hand movements. One parent described her way of coping with her child's flapping behavior:

> At age 6, our daughter Michelle was constantly flapping her arms. She seemed to like doing this more than anything else. Since there seemed to be nothing we could do to stop it, we decided to use it as a reward for completing her chores. After she finishes her chores, we give her pom-poms and tell her that she may "cheer." She holds the pom-poms and flaps her arms. This has brought the hand flapping under control, since it occurs only during the "cheering" sessions.

These parents were disturbed by Michelle's arm flapping and inability to focus on appropriate tasks. The pom-poms enabled her to flap her arms in a more conventional and controlled way. She learned to "flap" only when the pom-poms were available, thus eliminating the behavior in public places where it was inappropriate. More important, the pom-poms served as a reward for Michelle, which her parents used to motivate her to complete desirable tasks, such as chores. Thus, Michelle's parents took advantage of her hand flapping in order to achieve a positive goal.

Many parents have found that this is not always possible. Sometimes self-stimulatory behaviors can be reduced only by using external rewards. One group of researchers (Eason, White, & Newson, 1982) described a boy who liked to spin objects. They were able to teach him to play with toys instead of spinning objects by systematically rewarding the boy each time he touched a toy but did not spin it. A parent tells of how she used a punishment system in a similar way:

> Max, our 12-year-old son, had learned how to load and unload the dishwasher. However, it took him a long time to do this because he'd twirl glasses and silverware. I knew that he loved raisins, so I lined up 10 raisins and said, "No spinning, twirling, or flapping and you can have all these raisins." Anytime he did one of those things, I took away one raisin and he could see it go back in the box. The rules were clear. He soon became very efficient at this dishwasher chore. Now he gets money instead of raisins for chores performed well.

Max's habit of spinning and twirling things distracted him from completing tasks that he otherwise knew how to do. To keep his attention focused, his mother set up a punishment system in which he could clearly see that he would lose a raisin each time he spun or twirled something. His mother helped make the rules clear in a way that made sense to Max. As he got older and could wait longer and have a more abstract reward, she switched to money instead of food. She also concentrated on having him gain his reward instead of losing something each time. This helped keep him focused on the task at hand, and gradually was used with other chores.

Unfortunately, sometimes parents cannot find a reward that motivates their child to lessen his or her unusual behavior. In such cases it can be helpful to restructure environmental conditions, as illustrated in the next anecdote.

> Julie is 10 years old and has the annoying habit at the dinner table of tapping her brother's and sister's plates, glasses, and bowls with her fork or spoon. We don't want to have her eat ahead of time or take away her utensils because we want her to be able to eat independently along with the rest of the family. We have moved her to a school desk adjacent to and facing the table so that she is included in the family circle but does not annoy her siblings.

These parents were caught in a bind because Julie's tapping behavior occurred with eating utensils, which they could not take away from her without decreasing her independence. They were faced with the choice of excluding her from family meals or accepting her disturbing behavior. They chose to accept her tapping behavior, but to minimize the annoying effect it had on other family members. This made it easier for them to view Julie positively, and avoided a potential power struggle that might have occurred if they simply tried to eliminate the behavior. Another possible solution to this problem would be to use only paper dishes and plastic forks and spoons for Julie for a while and to cover the table with a tablecloth that would muffle the sound she liked to hear when tapping things.

INSISTENCE ON SAMENESS

Insistence on sameness refers to a child's tendency to perform activities exactly in the same way without spontaneous variations, or to cling to old and familiar objects. The child becomes anxious and upset when there are any changes in routines or schedules. These behaviors place severe restrictions on family life. The family is forced to follow a rigidly predictable schedule and to try to avoid any unexpected events or changes. Since the unexpected can never be completely avoided, this often means tantrums and real distress when the inevitable changes take place.

The inability to act spontaneously or make changes can produce feelings of pressure and tension within the home. Commonplace events such as replacing worn-out objects have to be thought about and planned for when coping with a person who is extremely resistant to change.

> Ernest, our 31-year-old son, becomes very upset when anything in our home is changed. For instance, when the clock stopped in his bedroom,

I had to make sure that he was gone before I replaced the old clock. When I replace an old clock or any familiar household object that is broken, I make sure it is with a new one that looks a lot like the old one. I make a point of not having it exactly the same so that he will get used to some degree of change. He accepts the new clock or other object if it is already in place when he gets home.

Ernest's trait of being resistant to change has carried into adulthood, and his parents have accepted this. They learned that it helped them to cope with Ernest's behavior if they could plan expected replacement of household objects so that the change was completed before Ernest came home. They also made the new object similar to the old. Planning for changes was somewhat inconvenient for the family, but not as disruptive as Ernest's upset behavior would have been. In Ernest's case, insistence on sameness appears to be a lifelong trait. Parents and researchers have found that other people can be helped to overcome this difficult trait (Rutter, 1978), particularly when the child is young.

Marty, age 13, is a stickler for time. His watch was once slower than the teacher's, which so upset him that he wouldn't leave school that day because "It wasn't time yet." The next day, I didn't let him wear his watch to school and told him he had to go by the teacher's time. Although he asks about his watch sometimes, he goes to school easily without it.

Marty had a special interest in time and insisted that all watches and clocks tell the same time because he was confused if two watches were different. His confusion and subsequent need for sameness caused him to become upset if his watch and someone else's watch showed different times. In the previous anecdote, Ernest's mother maintained a similar appearance in different clocks to reduce Ernest's upset at change. In Marty's case, differences in watches were more difficult to control, since he was likely to see clocks with different times at school. His mother recognized this and decided that Marty's upset behavior could best be avoided by removing his watch. This lessened his confusion because he no longer had to worry about his watch being the same as everyone else's.

Another mother chose instead to have her son wear his watch and synchronize his with the teacher's each morning so that the times were the same. Another family chose to teach their son to ask what time it was when he was confused about something that didn't happen at "his" time. They then taught him that in school, the rule is that the teacher's time is okay.

Another teacher reported that Paul, an 11-year-old boy who recently transferred to her class, was obsessed with going swimming, an activity she scheduled three times a week for her class. Paul searched for the swimming pool daily and ran away from her class to find it. The teacher prepared a picture schedule for him so that he would see and anticipate when it was time to go swimming. His running-away behavior stopped as the visual schedule helped him to gain independence from his obsession. Visual structure and transition places where the child is helped to learn change of school activities are important components in the TEACCH educational system (Schopler, Mesibov & Hearsey, 1995).

VERBAL RITUALS

Another common form of ritualized behavior is the repetition of favorite words, sounds, or songs. This can include asking the same question over and over again. Such repetitive behaviors not only can become tiresome, but also can interfere with social interaction. An adolescent girl described in one study habitually screamed, even when not upset (O'Brian & Azrin, 1972). Her therapists set up a highly structured schedule of daily tasks in which she was rewarded each time she completed a task without screaming repetitively. Her screams disappeared. A mother reports here on a different approach to handling her son's verbal rituals:

> At age 6, Larry had certain words that he said over and over again. Everyone was tired of hearing them and became annoyed at him. Those words became forbidden—Larry was not allowed to say them. I put all of them on a board, and *once* each day I took them out and let him read them. When the board was put away, he could not say them again until the board was brought out again the following day. I made another board with a list of words that he *could* say. His positive board was always available to him, and he could add words to it.

Larry's ritual of repeating words made other people angry at him. His mother made a rule that he could not say these words, and she provided a structure for helping him not to be frustrated by their prohibition while learning other words that he could say in their stead. Having the forbidden words on a board and being able to say them once a day gave Larry a predictable outlet. Having the positive alternatives also on a board helped prevent him from feeling frustrated by replacing what was forbidden with something that was permitted. This mother's sensitive understanding of her son's difficulty is noteworthy because she was able to recognize that he did not repeat words in order to annoy her. When she created a structure for avoiding the problem, and rules for when the behavior was and was not appropriate, Larry was able to make the requested change.

Another form of verbal rituals is repetitive questioning. Being asked the same question again and again is exasperating, especially when we think that the one asking the question already knows the answer. Sometimes such questioning is done to seek reassurance that a favorite event will occur or to attempt to clarify what will happen next. Two parents suggested similar solutions to this problem:

> David, age 38, is always asking when something will happen. Sometimes I think he already knows the answer and just wants to hear me say it again. I made a wall calendar marked with key dates and put it up in his room. Whenever he asks me when something will happen, I send him to the calendar to get the answer himself. This has markedly reduced his perseverative questioning.

> Our 14-year-old son, Willie, liked to ask the same question over and over again. He seemed to come up with a new question every few weeks. Since this was very tiresome for me, I learned to put the answer on a paper and paste it on the refrigerator. When he asked me the question, I told him to go to the refrigerator and find the answer. Since he was able to read, I could write out the answers. For children who can't read, pictures can be used in place of words.

Both David and Willie annoyed their parents by repeatedly asking the same question. The solutions their parents proposed provided visual ways of answering the questions. Telling their son to look at his calendar or written answer reduced parental frustrations and provided a means by which their child could independently find the answer to his question. David's calendar was always there for him to look at. His anxiety or confusion about when, or if, favorite events would occur was reduced by seeing them marked on the calendar. Willie's questions concerned whatever topic was important to him at the time. As in David's case, the written answer allowed him to have continuous access to the answer independent of adult availability. As a result, his confusion was easily reduced. Strength in visual processing applies frequently in people with autism, and is used as a major tool in structural teaching (Schopler, Mesibov, & Hearsey, 1995).

In most of the examples in this chapter, parents were able to find some positive aspect to their child's repetitive behavior, and they found ways to have the repetitive behavior work for, not against, the child. Parents were also resourceful in finding ways to bring the behavior under control so that it occurred only at specified times and in specific places. While such compromises between the child's special interests and the needs of the family or community are not obvious in every situation, they can be found most of the time once you know how to look.

REFERENCES

Aiken, J. M., & Salzberg, C. L. (1984). The effects of a sensory extinction procedure on stereotypic sounds of two autistic children. *Journal of Autism and Developmental Disorders, 14,* 291–299.

American Psychiatric Association. (1994). *Diagnostic and Statistical Manual of Mental Disorders* (4th ed.). Washington, DC: Author.

Breese, G. R., Mueller, R. A., & Schroeder, S. R. (1987). The neurochemical basis of symptoms in the Lesch-Nyhan syndrome: Relationship to central symptoms in other developmental disorders. In E. Schopler & G. Mesibov (Eds.), *Neurobiological aspects of autism* (pp. 145–160). New York: Plenum Press.

Eason, L. J., White, M. J., & Newson, C. (1982). Generalized reduction of self-stimulatory behavior: An effect of teaching appropriate play to autistic children. *Analysis and Intervention in Developmental Disabilities, 2,* 157–169.

Epstein, L. H., Doke, L. A., Satwaj, T. E., Sorrell, S., & Rimmer, B. (1974). Generality and side effects of overcorrection. *Journal of Applied Behavior Analysis, 7,* 385–390.

Foxx, R. M., & Azrin, N. H. (1973). The elimination of autistic self-stimulatory behavior by overcorrection. *Journal of Applied Behavior Analysis, 6,* 1–14.

Kanner, L. (1943). Autistic disturbances of affective contact. *Nervous Child, 2,* 217–250.

Kern, L., Koegel, R. L., & Dunlap, G. (1984). The influence of vigorous versus mild exercise on autistic stereotyped behaviors. *Journal of Autism and Developmental Disorders, 14,* 57–67.

O'Brian, F., & Azrin, N. H. (1972). Symptom reduction by functional displacement in a token economy. *Journal of Behavior Therapy and Experimental Psychiatry, 3,* 205–207.

Richmond, G. (1983). Evaluation of treatment for a hand-mouthing stereotype. *American Journal of Mental Deficiency, 44,* 667–669.

Rutter, M. (1978). Diagnosis and definition. In M. Rutter & E. Schopler (Eds.), *Autism: A reappraisal of concepts and treatment.* New York: Plenum Press.

Schopler, E., Mesibov, G. B., and Hearsey, K. A. (1995). Structured teaching in the TEACCH system. In E. Schopler & G. B. Mesibov (Eds.), *Learning and cognition in autism* (pp. 243–268). New York: Plenum Press.

3

Communication

A communication deficit is a defining feature of autism. Many people with autism do not speak, and those who do often fail to communicate clearly what they want or need. The inability to communicate their needs can be very frustrating, leading to withdrawal from other people and often contributing to behavior problems.

Children with autism or related disabilities also have severe difficulties in understanding language. As infants, they do not respond to their parents' speech. This lack of response is confusing and upsetting to parents because they feel that they are not making a meaningful connection with their child. Parents frequently suspect deafness and are puzzled when told that their child's hearing is normal.

PROBLEMS WITH UNDERSTANDING LANGUAGE

Many people with disabilities have difficulty understanding what is being said to them. Directions given in an unfamiliar setting or involving two or more ideas can be confusing to these children. Even as adults, some may have difficulty understanding abstract words or concepts. They may become confused easily if someone speaks too quickly or uses too many words. Parents note that their children may have trouble following directions unless given in simple terms, in a familiar setting, with visual cues (Schopler, Mesibov, & Hearsey, 1995).

Confusion over Too Many Words

Some autistic children become confused easily when spoken to in long sentences or with complex words. Normal children understand language by relating the words they hear with their observation of the social situation at hand. For infants, language comprehension involves connecting words to behaviors that they already understand, such as looking, acting, and imitating (Lord, 1985). When parents talk to infants, they are careful to use simple language. They usually speak in one word or in very short phrases and try to talk about only one behavior at a time. Words are often used to guide the child to look at a particular object. Professionals have found that similar strategies work to help autistic children understand language (Lord & Baker, 1977). Teachers learn to speak in phrases geared to the child's level of language. These could be simple words familiar to the child, such as "Go play," "Put," or "Time to eat." Furthermore, it is helpful to point to the things that you are talking about in order to help the child make the connection between the words and what the words mean. One parent described how she gradually developed a similar approach:

> Tommy never understood what I was saying to him. The words I used just seemed to be noise to him, so I decided that I needed to change the way I talked to him. One day, as we were getting ready to leave the house, I just said "coat" and pointed to his coat instead of saying "Tommy, would you please get your coat?" He looked at me for a second and then grabbed his coat. For the first time, at age 5, I think he really understood what I was saying to him. From then on, I knew how to talk to him so that he would understand me.

Tommy had a serious problem understanding language. When his mother spoke to him in full sentences, he was confused and failed to respond. His mother finally hit on the solution of using only one word (*coat*) and pointing to the coat while she spoke. This combination of simple speech and gestures helped Tommy understand her and became a successful strategy from then on. It is important to use an appropriate level of language. Communication should not be abbreviated more than necessary. The far more frequent cause of miscommunications is complex communication rather than excessively simple sentences.

Memory Problems

Many autistic children have good short-term memories and may be able to repeat phrases that they do not understand (Schopler, Reichler, & Lansing, 1980). A striking example is echolalia, or the repetition of the most recently heard or remembered passage. After a longer time lapse, autistic children often have difficulty retrieving phrases or directions from their long-term memory. This can happen even when parents use phrases that their child understands. Inconsistent memory can produce confusion for parents unaware of the problem.

Beth, age 7, was going to a school in a city 55 miles from our house two mornings a week. A few months later, she started going to another school two afternoons a week, though on different days. Beth appeared not to accept the second school, fussing the entire time we were there. We traveled the same four-lane highway to both schools but had to go about 10 miles farther to the second school. When we left home, I always told her to which school we were going. One day I told her at home, and I repeated telling her about the second school two more exits from the first school turnoff. After that Beth was just great! Her teacher asked what had happened, since she was so quiet. I realized that I had been telling her too far ahead of time, and she had forgotten what I'd told her by the time we reached the school (an hour's drive). She was fine from that day on, and I always told her to which school we were going when we got close to the turnoff.

On the surface, this child was upset by the change in her routine of going to the first school. Her mother's intuitive understanding of Beth's upset feeling enabled her to use a different approach and to warn Beth well in advance about the upcoming disturbing change in routine. When her mother realized that Beth's problem was a difficulty in long-term memory rather than resistance to change, she repeated her message about a change just before it was going to happen. This lessened Beth's confusion, increased her motivation to attend school, and led to improved behavior.

Visual aids may also be used to help children with memory problems. Children can be given a written message, a picture, or an object that will help them remember something they are supposed to do, or remind them of an impending change (Watson, Lord, Schaffer, & Schopler, 1989). For example, the mother in the preceding anecdote might have given her daughter a written message or a picture of the teacher at the second school to remind her to which school they were going that day. This type of cuing is illustrated by the following anecdote:

I find that it helps my 9-year-old son, Matt, if I use written words to reinforce what I am saying to him. He understands written words much better than he understands speech. For instance, recently Matt got out of bed throughout one night. The next morning he asked for Jell-O for breakfast. I said no because he hadn't stayed in bed during the night, but that he could have Jell-O after school. I wrote him a note that said, "Matt will go to school. When he comes home he will eat Jell-O." With this, he understood the situation. There was no tantrum, and he stayed in bed the next night.

Without the written note, Matt probably would have forgotten his mother's message and become upset. The written words gave him time to think about their meaning and thus prevented his confusion. Also, unlike spoken language, the message lasted all day and was there for the boy to look at repeatedly. Pictures can be used for the same purpose. The advantage written words have over pictures is that more complicated messages can be communicated.

Reducing Auditory Processing Problems

Many children with autism perform better on visual tasks than on auditory tasks (Fulwiler & Fouts, 1976; Lancioni, 1983; Mesibov, Schopler, & Hearsey, 1994; Schopler, Mesibov, & Hearsey, 1995). This is one of the main reasons for training people with autism to use visually oriented communication systems such as objects, picture cards, sign language, letter boards, and written words. Given the difficulties autistic people often have understanding language, both parents and professionals have found it helpful to use visual aids to explain directions and upcoming events. For example, to explain what will happen that day, many teachers train their students to read and follow schedules. Schedules do not always need to involve words. For those students who cannot read, schedules can be color-coded, or objects can be used to represent a particular activity, thus preventing countless behavior problems and enabling the children to know what will happen next. A teacher writes:

> Janice is a nonverbal, low-functioning 18-year-old who becomes confused during transitions from one situation to another. She doesn't know where to go unless we constantly remind her or physically guide her to the appropriate place. She likes photos, so we have taken pictures of all the different places the class goes and the activities they do. Whenever

the class is getting ready to go someplace, I show Janice a picture of that place so that she understands what is going to happen next. This helps lessen her confusion and enables her to be more independent during transitions.

Janice is not able to understand changes in setting from verbal description alone. The photos provide her with a constant visual reminder of where she is going next. With this cue in front of her, her confusion is decreased. Her motivation to go to new places with the rest of her class was visibly improved.

Failure to Generalize Meaning

Many people with autism are unable to generalize word meaning. A word understood in one situation may be meaningless to the person in a different situation. Part of this problem involves the way in which the autistic person came to understand the word in the first place. Instead of understanding a word according to its broad meaning, a child may have picked up on cues to its meaning in only one narrow circumstance. This is illustrated by the following example:

> In our house, we have one room that is set up for Luis, our 6-year-old son, to play in. It is very safe, and there is nothing he can break in there. Whenever Luis has free time and I need to do something else, I tell him "Go play," and he knows he should go in that room and play with his toys. One day I took him to the town park and told him to "Go play." Instead of going to the swings, he just flapped his hands in the air. I realized that he didn't really understand the word *play*. I began to take him to the park every day, and after I said "Go play," I would lead him to the swings or climbing bars. Gradually, he came to understand "Go play" as soon as we got out of the car at the park.

Luis's mother had overestimated his language comprehension because he responded appropriately to "Go play" within the house. Her son thought that "Go play" meant he should go to his room and play with his toys. In another setting, the same words did not have any meaning. His mother taught him the meaning of "Go play" by leading him to play objects every time she gave the command. Gradually, he learned to "go play" at the park as well as at home. The meaning of *play* at a friend's or a relative's house might again have to be taught separately.

PROBLEMS WITH EXPRESSING LANGUAGE

Since many autistic children speak little or not at all, it is often necessary to teach them alternative communication systems (Watson et al, 1989; Wilbur, 1985). In the past, some experts believed that teaching alternative communication systems would inhibit the child's learning of verbal communication. But current research and teaching experience indicate that this is not usually the case. On the contrary, many children with autism improve in verbal skills at the same time they are learning alternative systems.

Many developmentally disabled people need visual cues in order to communicate. Unless they can see the object for which a word stands, they have difficulty recalling that word. Unable to visualize what happened somewhere else, such children cannot answer their parents' questions about what they did in school that day.

Lack of awareness of social conventions also causes many communication problems. Most parents of young children have been embarrassed when their child blurted out something in public that should have been spoken in private. For parents of autistic children, such an event may be commonplace even when their children are older. Failure to perceive social conventions may lead a young person needing help in a store to yell out, "Hey, clerk!" Sometimes the person talks too loudly or too softly, oblivious to the effect that speech volume has on other people. A more verbal person may talk endlessly about a single topic or ask repetitive questions.

Need for an Alternative System

Many parents eventually reach a point where they decide that their children must have some way of communicating, whether or not they can speak. However, it is not always easy to decide which alternative system is best for a given child. When selecting an alternative system, it is important to weigh the advantages and the limitations of a particular system and compare these characteristics to the child's strengths and weaknesses. For example, a child who thinks slowly and is visually oriented may do very well using a picture system. However, a hyperactive child who is constantly fidgeting and jumping from place to place may need a system that is easily portable, like gestures or a picture cards booklet. One also should look at the child's everyday life and decide which systems are feasible and used for spontaneous language. These should be incorporated into situations that the child is in most frequently, and form the basis of teaching communication skills (Watson et al., 1989). Parents often select communication systems based on particular skills. Sometimes, however, the selection develops quite unintentionally through a skill not initially thought of for communication.

> Tommy had little language but started showing an interest in written words by age 8. So I bought him a "Speak and Spell" that had a function where a word would appear on a screen, and the machine would say the word. Tommy learned to spell every word in the "Speak and Spell." I told his teacher about this. She began writing out words and phrases that he would need, like "I want to go to the bathroom." When he wanted to do something, he had to get the sign, take it to the teacher, and read it to her. Gradually the signs were faded out, and now he can say what he wants without reading a card.

Although Tommy was unable to speak, he had excellent visual discrimination skills, as demonstrated by the ease with which he learned to read and spell. His mother picked up on this strength and on his interest in written words. The teacher transformed this ability to read and spell into a communication system by writing out phrases that he needed to satisfy common needs and wants.

Teaching an alternative system is generally more painstaking than it was for Tommy. Usually, the system has to be broken down into small steps that the child learns one at a time. Benaroya, Wesley, Oglvie, Klien, and Meany (1977) found that teaching autistic children sign language was difficult because they did not imitate well and avoided eye contact. These researchers began by tickling children just enough to help them notice another person. Slowly, they were able to get the children to copy their body movements. Over time, they shaped these body movements into sign language and paired the sign with an object. Carrier (1974) and Lancioni (1983) both found that before teaching an autistic child to communicate using pictures, they had to teach the child to match simple objects to pictures. Over time, the child came to understand what the pictures represented without having to see the object. At this stage, the child was trained to point to a picture in order to receive what he or she wanted. A mother reports her own picture system:

> I felt a great sadness that David could not or would not talk. By the time David was 6, it became very important to David's father and me that David have some means of communication. We decided to try a picture system because he seemed to understand things he could see. When he was 6, I began to make 3 × 5 cards with both the picture and the name for every article in our house. I taped the cards to the place where he would find the item: food cards to the refrigerator, clothes cards to the closet, and so on. We started a "Find the card to answer the question" game. To get what he wanted, David had to find the right card. Soon he would come to me with a picture on his own initiative in order to get what he wanted.

David's mother spent a good deal of time and energy teaching her son an alternative system of communication. She used pictures that were meaningful to him because they involved common household items and foods he wanted. The system worked because it focused on objects that were motivating to the boy and also because his visual skills were better than his auditory and verbal skills. Next is another parent's example of creating a picture system for a nonverbal boy:

> My 10-year-old son, Rami, is totally nonverbal. To help him communicate, we made a communication book with pictures in it for him. He has to point to the pictures to get items he wants or needs. When dressing in the morning, we both point to pictures of a shirt, pants, and so on, and he goes to his drawer to get those items. Since this system has worked so well, we have begun to use it at other times of the day, such as mealtime and bathtime.

Many classroom teachers use communication books. The books are especially useful for children who enjoy looking at them and understand pictures of familiar items. All of the child's pictures can be consolidated in one book. Rami's mother combined the use of a picture book with common, everyday activities such as dressing, eating, and bathing. This ensured that communication practice would take place daily. Since communication practice was combined with a self-help skill, it was not time consuming for the parent.

Parents frequently ask "How will an alternative communication system work?" The two previous examples of picture systems were successful within the home but could be impractical in the community. This problem increases as the child learns to use more pictures and the picture system becomes cumbersome. An efficient solution to this difficulty is suggested by one creative parent:

> My 8-year-old son cannot talk. Sometimes Ken can let family members know what he wants, but other people have trouble figuring out what he wants. I began taking Polaroid pictures of things that he liked, such as his favorite foods. Whenever he wanted something, I made him show me the picture of it. Once he got used to this system, I wanted him to be able to use it with other people. I made him a ring (on his belt) and attached his pictures to it. Now Ken has several rings that are used for different trips, such as eating fast food, going to the mall, or taking the bus.

This parent solved several problems. First, she worked around her son's language handicap and gradually trained him to communicate by showing her pictures. Second, by placing the ring of pictures on his belt, Ken's mother made it possible for him to communicate in a variety of places with a variety of people. This solved the previous problem of most people not understanding what Ken wanted. Third, by creating different rings for different situations, she enabled Ken to greatly expand the use of this system. If she had tried to put too many pictures on a single ring, the system would have been too complicated, and Ken would have become confused.

The following parent mentions a common problem: that autistic people have difficulty communicating with unfamiliar people. Picture systems are readily understood by everyone. This eliminates one of the major criticisms of sign language, which is that it is not understood by the general public. The usefulness of picture systems with the general public becomes especially important as students get older and are out in the community more.

> Sandy is a 16-year-old nonverbal male who has difficulty expressing his wants and needs to others. He has no way of communicating other than sign language, which few people other than family and teachers understand. His teachers, mother, speech therapist, and consultants met and devised a picture communication system. He now has eight Polaroid

pictures that he carries on a ring attached to his belt. Among Sandy's pictures are his favorite food, which he selects in the cafeteria at school, and bowling shoes, which he uses to get his own shoes when he goes bowling each week. The number of pictures will increase as he becomes more familiar with the system.

Sandy's ability to communicate was limited while sign language was his only communication system. The important adults in his life met and decided that a picture system would better suit his needs. This portable and readily understood system allowed him to communicate with people in the community. His teacher selected pictures based on his favorite activities, which helped motivate him to use the new system.

Sometimes a communication system may not work because of a child's limitations rather than limitations of the system itself. One important possibility is to adapt the system by making it simpler before trying a new communication system, as illustrated in the following example:

> Ted, age 13, communicated only through sign language. He was having difficulty learning the sign and meaning of "no," so his teachers decided to teach him "stop" instead. The sign for "stop" involves one hand hitting the other and is simpler and more active than the sign for "no." It also seemed that the sign for "stop" had more meaning for Ted, since many times when he communicated "no," his actual need was to get someone to "stop" bothering him.

Instead of abandoning sign language and finding an alternative system, these teachers made the act of signing more meaningful for Ted. Signing "stop" was physically easier for Ted than signing "no," and thus he was more likely to use it. The meaning of the sign for "stop" was more direct than that for "no," which helped it to make more sense to him. Further, signing "stop" helped Ted get the desired response from the other students, and thus helped to motivate his social interactions.

Frustrations from the Inability to Communicate

Both parents and professionals have observed that children who lack a communication system are often unnecessarily frustrated and likely to have behavior problems. Research backs up this commonsense conclusion. Noncommunicative retarded people have been observed to show more aggressive behaviors than people with a useful communication system. Children who cannot communicate effectively may have difficulty gaining attention appropriately and thus may resort to attention-seeking behavior. Carr and Durand (1985) trained students who engaged in attention- seeking behavior to communicate appropriately to get their teacher's attention. They found that behavior problems were substantially reduced and that the students remained on-task for longer periods of time. Parents report similar results after their children learned to communicate effectively.

> My daughter Anna was unable to speak but desperately wanted to communicate. This left her frustrated and sometimes led to behavior problems or aggression. When Anna was 5 years old, I persuaded her school to teach her sign language. She learned 300 signs in 6 months. We found that her frustration level and aggression dropped dramatically at this point, as her desire to communicate increased.

Another mother found a similar result:

> My 9-year-old son, Sean, was unable to tell us what he wanted except through pointing and making sounds. He became upset when we couldn't figure out what he wanted. I learned sign language because Sean was learning it at school. When he used signs, he had fewer tantrums because he was able to get what he wanted.

In both cases, the child unable to communicate was frustrated and angry. Once these children learned sign language and were able to communicate what they wanted in a way that could be clearly understood, their behavior improved noticeably. It was especially important for the parents to learn sign language and use it at home. This helped their children generalize their communication skills from school to home.

Difficulties Communicating in Different Environments

Communicating about something not present in the immediate environment is difficult for many people with autism. This is due partly to their inability to form a mental picture of something that they cannot see right then. Generally, such individuals depend on being able to see something in order to be able to talk about it. This makes it difficult for them to transmit information from one place to another, such as from home to school.

> Roger, our 10-year-old, is not able to tell us what happened in school, though we ask him questions repeatedly. His teacher gave him a diary that she writes in every day to describe what he did in school that day. Now that Roger has learned how to write, she has him write in the diary before he leaves school in the afternoon. We have also started having him write in the diary before he goes to school in the morning, to describe what he did at home the night before. This builds a meaningful connection between home and school. It helps people at school to elicit language from him because they know a little about what he's been doing when he's not with them.

Without the diary, Roger either was not able to remember or was not able to visualize what happened earlier that day. As his mother pointed out, the diary provided a link between his two most important environments and helped people to motivate communication from him. Roger had the added advantage of being able to write in the diary himself. This made the elicited conversation even more meaningful to him because he was the one who wrote the information down. Thus, the diary enabled the boy to communicate across two environments, which he otherwise would not have been able to do. Another parent described a similar idea that helped his son communicate information across two places:

> When David was younger, around age 10, he had no way of telling us what had happened in school. He didn't know how to write, but had very good hand–eye coordination and perceptual discrimination skills. One of his teachers discovered that he could form each letter of the alphabet perfectly, so she would have him tell her what he wanted to say to his parents. Then she would write this out in sentence form, and he would copy it. By making the most of the skills David had, his teacher helped him to communicate with his parents. He still uses this technique of letter writing today, though now he has learned to write his own letters.

Although David was verbal, he was unable to remember enough to be able to tell his parents what had happened in school. His teacher transformed his skill of copying letters into a means of communicating with his parents. Thus, a communication problem was solved by capitalizing on his strong fine-motor and perceptual skills.

Lack of Social Communication

People with autism who have gained a communication system and can be understood by others often still have other communication problems. Two problems that parents frequently mention are the inability to express feelings and the lack of conversational ability. These problems involve impairment of both social and communication skills, the primary features of autism. Autistic people often do not show much interest in chatting or in talking simply for the pleasure of interacting with someone else. Instead, their communication is focused on satisfying a need or gaining information. This lack of social interaction frequently sets the autistic person apart from other handicapped people and is a source of concern to parents.

> Karl was able to communicate what he wanted, but his speech was rote and stilted. We always hoped he would learn to talk in a more natural way. When Karl was 21 years old, he started making spontaneous comments for the first time. Anytime he would make such a comment, we would respond very positively. We tried to build a conversation around the comment by asking him questions about what he had said. He now is able to sustain a 15-minute conversation and makes spontaneous comments daily.

Karl was verbal for many years before he began to chat. His parents used natural, positive reinforcement to reward their son for talking. They helped make his comments more social by elaborating on them with questions. This showed their interest and began to teach him about the back-and-forth nature of conversations, or turn taking. Turn taking is the building block of successful conversation, but it is also a skill that is difficult for many autistic people. Beisler and Tsai (1983) reported that most autistic children have not learned to establish a common focus or take turns during conversation. This makes a great deal of their speech one-sided. To teach developmentally disabled people how to take turns, some professionals have used normal children as role models, which seems to work best under adult supervision (Mesibov, 1992).

Many parents complain that their autistic child cannot express his or her feelings. This can frustrate both child and parent. Parents often worry that their child may be in physical pain but cannot express it. One approach to teaching children how to express their feelings is to teach names of feelings with pictures of different facial expressions. This may be difficult for some children to understand if the label is not directly linked to feelings being experienced at that particular time. One of the most successful methods is to label an emotion at the time the child is clearly showing it.

> When our 6-year-old son, Jim, began to tantrum, we coached him to use words to express what he is feeling. We said to him, "You're really mad because you wanted that toy. It is okay to say that you are mad." Generally, he is able to follow our suggestion, which makes his tantrums shorter and less frequent.

This anecdote brings out several important points. First, his parents were able to make saying "I am mad" meaningful to Jim by capturing the moment in which he really was mad. Having him label his emotion while he was actually feeling it enabled him to make the connection between the word and the feeling. Second, these parents reinforced their son for talking about his feelings rather than tantruming. They told him that talking about his feelings was all right. This provided an outlet for him, which served to calm him down and decrease his tantrums.

Social Rule Deficits

Autistic children sometimes appear inhibited in public places because they lack understanding of social rules. For example, they may be unaware that behavioral expectations are different in church than in a shopping mall. This can cause embarrassment for their parents. Sometimes, this behavior is severe enough to prevent a family from going to public places.

> We like to attend a weekly Friends Meeting. This service is primarily silent. We wanted to take our son David, but whenever it occurred to him to say something, he'd say it—at full volume. Gradually, we realized that David had never learned to whisper. So we taught him how to whisper, and found that he enjoyed it. Now we can all go to the Friends Meeting, and David is no longer disruptive.

Characteristically, David did not understand rules of behavior in a particular social situation. Instead of preventing him from attending the service, his parents taught him to whisper. Once David learned to whisper, he could talk without disturbing others at the meeting, and his parents could attend the service without fear of embarrassment.

Autistic people may be unaware that their behavior is disturbing someone else, since they have difficulty taking another person's perspective. In terms of controlling voice volume, they may talk too loudly or too softly and fail to perceive why that would matter to anyone else. Nonhandicapped children may be helpful in modeling appropriate voice volume. They can help autistic children enjoy interactions and improve their ability to speak at a reasonable volume.

The failure to read social situations appropriately can lead to embarrassing behavior in other ways. Some autistic children do not distinguish familiar people from strangers or at least do not behave differently with strangers than with familiar people.

> When out in public, my 8-year-old son, Jack, would often go up and begin talking to strangers. Sometimes he would run on and on about something that interested him but that the poor stranger couldn't care less about. So we taught him to say only "Good morning" or "Good afternoon." It seemed he wanted some contact, and this greeting seemed to satisfy him.

Jack's running on about a topic of interest only to himself was clearly socially inappropriate. There is also the risk that a stranger may exploit such a naive person. Jack's parents realized that he could not understand either that he might be boring to someone or that a stranger could pose a potential danger. Their idea of a greeting was an excellent compromise. This satisfied his need for contact while preventing embarrassing or troublesome behaviors. Jack was rewarded for making a single greeting and stopping there.

People with autism are also unaware that certain words or topics of conversation are inappropriate when discussed in public. A parent gave the following example:

> Our 12-year-old daughter, Jean, had the bad habit of swearing when she was angry. We were unable to get her to learn that this was socially undesirable. Finally, we decided to teach her substitute expressions that were acceptable. These substitute expressions sounded similar to the

swear words (e.g., "Golly day" for "God damn"), which made it easier to get her to use them. She now uses these expressions instead of the swear words.

Jean was expressing her feelings, but in a socially unattractive style. Her parents realized that she was unable to recognize her behavior as undesirable. They worked around this problem by teaching her substitute phrases. She learned these quickly because they sounded like the expressions she was already using and they provided the same purpose, giving her an outlet for her anger.

Parents of nonverbal and poorly communicating children sometimes fear that their child may get lost while out in the community.

> My 19-year-old autistic son, Jason, is nonverbal. Although he knows a few signs, he cannot give his name and address if he is lost. We came up with the idea of giving him an ID card and teaching him to show it to people when they asked for his name. The Division of Motor Vehicles provided a license-like ID with a picture for a small fee. The ID was clear, understandable, and especially age-appropriate for older children. Since Jason has learned to use the ID, we are not as nervous about letting him be independent in public places.

Many parents and teachers have developed the idea of providing developmentally disabled people with an ID card or a bracelet that they are trained to show to people in response to specific questions, such as "What is your name?" or "Where do you live?" The IDs can be readily interpreted by anyone and provide useful emergency information such as name, phone number, address, and parents' names.

SUMMARY
In this chapter, we discussed anecdotes covering two broad categories of communication: problems with understanding and difficulty with expressive language. Problems of understanding include confusion over too many words, memory problems, inability to process auditory information without visual cues, and failure to generalize meanings. For problems of expressive language, we discussed the use of alternative systems and frustration over communication difficulties in different environments. We also discussed anecdotes dealing with the lack of social communication and social rule deficits.

REFERENCES

Beisler, J. M., & Tsai, L. Y. (1983). A pragmatic approach to increase expressive language skills in young autistic children. *Journal of Autism and Developmental Disorders, 13,* 287–303.

Benaroya, S., Wesley, S., Oglvie, H., Klien, L. S., & Meany, M. (1977). Sign language and multisensory input training of children with communication and developmental disorders. *Journal of Autism and Childhood Schizophrenia, 7,* 23–31.

Carr, E., & Durand, V. M. (1985). Reducing behavior problems through functional communication training. *Journal of Applied Behavior Analysis, 18,* 111–126.

Carrier, J. K., Jr. (1974). Nonspeech noun usage training with severely and profoundly retarded children. *Journal of Speech and Hearing Research, 17,* 510–517.

Coleman, S. L., & Steadman, J. M. (1974). Use of a peer model in language training in an echolalic child. *Journal of Behavior Therapy and Experimental Psychiatry, 5,* 275–279.

Fulwiler, R. L., & Fouts, R. S. (1976). Acquisition of American Sign Language by a noncommunicative autistic child. *Journal of Autism and Childhood Schizophrenia, 6,* 43–51.

Lancioni, G. E. (1983). Using pictorial representations as communication means with low- functioning children. *Journal of Autism and Developmental Disorders, 13,* 87–106.

Lord, C. (1985). Autism and the comprehension of language. In E. Schopler & G. B. Mesibov (Eds.), *Communication problems in autism* (pp. 256–282). New York: Plenum Press.

Lord, C., & Baker, A. (1977). Communicating with autistic children. *Journal of Pediatric Psychology, 2,* 181–186.

Mesibov, G. B. (1992). Treatment issues with high-functioning adolescents and adults with autism. In E. Schopler & G. B. Mesibov (Eds.), *High functioning individuals with autism* (pp. 143–155). New York: Plenum Press.

Mesibov, G., Schopler, E., & Hearsey, K. (1994). Structured teaching. In E. Schopler & G. Mesibov (Eds.), *Behavioral management in autism* (pp. 195–210). New York: Plenum Press.

Schopler, E. (1994). Neurobiologic correlates in the classification and study of autism. In S. Broman & J. Grafman (Eds.), *Atypical cognitive deficits in developmental disorders: Implications for brain function.* Hillsdale, NJ: Lawrence Erlbaum.

Schopler, E., Mesibov, G. B., & Hearsey, K. A. (1995). Structured teaching in the TEACCH system. In E. Schopler & G. B. Mesibov (Eds.), *Learning and Cognition in Autism* (pp. 243–268). New York: Plenum Press.

Schopler, E., Reichler, R., & Lansing, M. (1980). *Individualized assessment and treatment for autistic and developmentally disabled children. Volume II: Teaching strategies for parents and professionals.* Baltimore: University Park Press.

Talkington, L. W., Hall, S., & Altman, R. (1971). Communication deficits and aggression in the mentally retarded. *American Journal of Mental Deficiency, 76,* 235–237.

Watson, L., Lord, C., Schaffer, B., & Schopler, E. (1989). *Teaching spontaneous communication to autistic and developmentally handicapped children.* Austin, TX: Pro- Ed.

Wilbur, R. B. (1985). Sign language and autism. In E. Schopler & G. B. Mesibov (Eds.), *Communication problems in autism* (pp. 229–253). New York: Plenum Press.

4

Play and Leisure

**Problem
Behaviors**

**Underlying
Deficits**

For young children, playing with toys and with other children is usually as natural as breathing. Most children prefer the company of other children to being alone. Even infants usually prefer the human voice over other sounds and choose pictures of human faces over other pictures or patterns. For children or adults with autism or similar developmental disorders, however, these same natural activities become difficult tasks they have to master. In fact, difficulty with social interaction and representational play is one of the identifying characteristics in the definition of autism (American Psychiatric Association, 1994; National Society for Autistic Children, 1977). Children with autism often respond to common toys by tasting, banging, or spinning them. They often lack the ability to pretend-play or imitate others. They may not have a sense of winning or losing, and they often seem to be indifferent or even hostile to playing with different toys or other children.

Parents and teachers gave many examples of difficulties their children or students had with play and leisure time: engaging in self-stimulation when not involved in an adult-directed activity, playing repetitively with one toy when there were many interesting ones to choose from, and being left out or made fun of by neighborhood children because of odd behaviors and lack of social and cooperative play skills. Families reported staying at home instead of going out because their child lacked leisure skills usable in the community. Our experience also suggests that an adult with autism is more likely to lose a job because he or she doesn't know how to use break and lunch time appropriately than because he or she doesn't have the job skills.

On the other hand, children with autism and similar developmental disabilities can and do learn to enjoy themselves. Often they need to be taught both the *desire* to play and the *skills* needed to do so. Although some school personnel may think of teaching play or leisure as frivolous, it should be a critical focus of any individualized education plan. First, the ability to play, to have fun, is a simple human right. Learning to play independently also relieves stress on parents and other caretakers, and leisure time gives children and adults interests and activities they can share with their nonhandicapped peers. This means they will be more apt to be welcomed and included in activities with brothers and sisters or with other children in the school and the neighborhood.

Children who learn to enjoy the public library or the community swimming pool are more likely to have pleasurable encounters with others and so improve their social skills. Building community leisure skills for the family member with autism also gives other family members opportunities to enjoy vacations and other "normal" family recreations. These are more important than is often recognized by adults trained and commited to the work ethic.

LEARNING TO LIKE PLAY AND LEISURE

Parents are often quick to recognize that before they can teach their child play skills, the child has to learn to *like* to play with particular toys, activities, or other children. One mother reported her frustration at having her 3-year-old son ignore his shiny new wagon:

> We got my autistic 3-year-old son, Justin, a beautiful red wagon for Christmas. The day after the holiday, he just ignored it and continued his usual running and pacing through the house. I tried just putting him in the wagon, but he jumped out and ran off. He does love to be tickled though, so I came up with a plan with his brother Mark's help. I put Justin in the wagon and tickled him briefly while his brother started to pull the wagon before Justin could get out. Mark pulled Justin in a small circle around me. Each time Justin went by, I tickled him while the wagon was still moving. He loved it and would come and take Mark and me to play the game. Soon Mark could both pull and tickle him. Before long, Justin learned to like the wagon ride without any tickling. His brothers and sisters take him for rides in the neighborhood now, and Justin is starting to get interested in pulling other people in the wagon.

Justin's mother recognized that he had no interest in playing with his wagon, so she used her knowledge of what Justin liked in order to teach him a useful play behavior. She paired tickling, which he did like, with rides in the wagon. Eventually she was able to gradually reduce the tickling. This resulted in an enjoyable activity for Justin, a way for his brothers and sisters to interact with him in the neighborhood, and an activity that lends itself to including other children.

Similarly, another mother taught her child to learn to enjoy rocking in a rocking chair.

> My 2-year-old son, Tom, was a blur of constant motion. He would never cuddle or sit in my lap or even sit by himself in a rocking chair. Since he liked to be "on the go," I started picking him up and holding him loosely while I quickly danced and sang around the room. I didn't hold him very long at first—just a few swoops around the room. Gradually, I could increase the dancing and singing time, and he let me hold him more closely while we danced. Soon I could hold him in the rocking chair if I sang the "dancing song" and moved the rocker quickly. It was nice to be able to sit down because he is a big boy and was getting very heavy. Soon he would climb up in the rocking chair and rock himself if he was tired or upset about something.

Tom's mother decided that he could enjoy physical contact and rocking if he'd only allow himself to experience it. She paired holding with the motion Tom liked so much, and she ended up teaching him to rock in the chair and comfort himself when he was upset.

Sometimes this pairing technique can be used to introduce interaction with other children.

> Raymond, age 3, liked the teacher to pick him up, but did not want other children to join him in any activities. His teacher first taught him to enjoy contact with her by swinging him in the air and then bouncing him on her knees while she recited a nursery rhyme. Once Raymond learned to like the knee bouncing and would regularly initiate the game, the teacher expanded the game to include another child. At this point, the teacher bounced Raymond only when another child was also on her knees. Raymond would then go and get his "bouncing partner" in order to play the game. At first, Raymond just ignored the other child while they bounced, but eventually would laugh with him and seek him out for other shared activities.

Here the other child became Raymond's "ticket" to an activity he enjoyed. Gradually, he learned to enjoy the child's company. A less athletic teacher could substitute shared wagon rides or other favored activities for the knee-bouncing game. Sometimes a one-to-one time is needed to overcome fears about a play activity.

> Roger, a 5-year-old in my class, was afraid of swinging. I decided to slowly get him used to swinging. I would swing him once in my lap, doing this five times a day. After 2 months, he was willing to swing alone and seemed to enjoy it. He comes and gets me to put him on the swing now.

The teacher decided that swinging could eventually become a pleasurable play activity for Roger. She made him go through with the swinging activity, but was sensitive enough to realize that he would need much reassurance, and so proceeded in small steps. This was done in a comforting one-to-one time.

An example similar to the preceding one comes from a family who was disappointed when their son did not at first share their enthusiasm for boating.

> When Mark was 2½, we took a family vacation to a lake for a week. We took along our boat, as we are great fishing and boating enthusiasts.
>
> The first evening we decided to go for a family boat ride. As we set out across the lake, Mark started screaming at the top of his lungs. We tried everything to soothe him, but nothing worked. We finally returned to shore in desperation.
>
> We knew he wasn't afraid of the motor noises. He had never startled at loud noises. (In fact, shortly after that he was diagnosed as having a "severe hearing loss," which was erroneous.)
>
> The next evening I held him very tightly on my lap and sang to him and hugged him. We decided we would ride for 20 minutes exactly. We did the same thing the next night, always holding him very tightly and comforting him, and riding only 20 minutes.
>
> By the end of the week there were no more tears. Now, at 13, he's always the first one in the boat.

Because this family wanted Mark to enjoy boating, they made boating experiences as pleasurable as possible. The singing, the comforting one-to-one on a parent's lap, and the brevity of the first few rides all helped Mark's fears subside and interest build. There were probably a few anxious experiences, but the eventual result led to less stressful vacations for the family and gave them an activity they could all enjoy together.

One father took a similar approach to the family swimming pool:

> We finally were able to build the family pool. For safety reasons, everyone in the family needed to develop some swimming skills. However, I was especially worried about my 18-year-old autistic son, Dean. I finally taught him to swim by getting right in the water with him. I showed him what to do and moved his body through the motions over and over until he could do it, first with a few words of encouragement and then on his own. Dean is not an expert swimmer, but he loves the water now. I worry less about his safety in the water now. He can also join in appropriately when friends come to swim.

This father showed patience and perseverance in physically guiding his son in learning to swim. Even with a specific play or leisure environment and materials, most autistic children do not automatically acquire the needed play and leisure skills. They have to be taught directly and systematically at first. As with teaching other areas of development, play and leisure skills can best be taught by breaking skills down into small steps and teaching each small step in sequence. In Dean's case, the motions needed by the different body parts were taught separately in small steps. Physically guiding Dean through the steps probably helped him to better understand what was expected. His father also modeled what to do with his own swimming and gave Dean verbal cues to remind him of the sequence after he had mastered the separate steps in the swimming process. Now Dean has a rewarding leisure activity, and his father has some peace of mind when Dean is near the pool.

CHANGING THE GAME FOR SUCCESS

Children or adults with developmental disabilities may not enjoy particular activities because they are not successful at them. Sometimes changing the equipment, the rules, or the order in which the activities are done can make a dramatic difference in the individual's enjoyment.

> Melissa has some physical coordination problems in addition to her autism. I was pleased that she was going to the bowling alley with a

group of young adults. I thought the exercise as well as the company would be good for her. However, she found the bowling so confusing and difficult and did so badly that she started flapping and whooping until everyone in the place was staring. The next time they went, someone brought a 3-foot-long aluminum ball chute that was set up at the line. Melissa didn't have to measure out her steps and swing the ball back, which was difficult for her. She just set it on the chute and pushed. It rolled and knocked down rows of pins to the shouts and cheers of her group. Melissa was high scorer for the night. Now she looks forward to bowling, and the only gestures she has are "high fives" with a buddy when she bowls the pins over.

No one likes an activity in which there is no chance of success. A considerate person in the bowling group adapted the skill level needed to accommodate Melissa's limitations. She was then free to enjoy the success of bowling and the supportive company of her cheering peers.

Here is another example of adapting equipment:

Our son Danny, who is 5, does not like a traditional swing because his feet don't touch the ground when he is in it. He can't move the swing by himself and feels uncomfortable when someone is pushing him and he can't stop the swing himself. So we hung a tire swing that he can lay across and propel with his feet still on the ground. He loves it!

Swinging was frightening for Danny because he was not in control of making the swing move or stop. After his parents adapted the swing, Danny enjoyed swinging more because his feet touched the ground and he was in control of the swing. He could also be more independent.

Parents have always modified game rules for younger family members by moving the child closer to a throwing target such as a basketball hoop, a beanbag target, or a dart board. Sometimes, even individualized rule changes are helpful in adjusting an activity.

My son Dwight really wanted to play softball with his older brother, Mike, but he couldn't throw or catch well enough, and he could never hit the ball with the bat. He would fuss and whine when the kids wouldn't let him play. One day Mike told him that if he didn't talk to or touch the runner, he could run to the first-base coaching box every time there was a hit. Now when the older kids get a hit, he races along outside the baseline to the coach's box. He's really picking up speed, and the kids don't mind having him around now that he doesn't whine. They even practice playing catch with him now, so it won't be too long until he'll really be able to play ball (or join a running team) with kids his own age.

This brother was patient enough to find a way to involve Dwight in the baseball game and make it more enjoyable for both of them. Other rule adjustments that parents and teachers suggested included having everyone on the side get a turn at bat instead of retiring the side after the customary three outs.

Table games and other less active games can also be adapted so that they are easier to take part in but still enjoyable for everyone who wants to participate.

Bob, our 10-year-old autistic son, is the youngest of three closely aged children. The two older siblings often involve him in their games and activities by changing the rules or leaving out the parts that are too difficult for him. For example, in the commercial game "Sorry," a move can be split between two tokens—the number 7 can be completed by moving one token 3 and another token 4. When Bob is playing, everyone completes his or her move with one token only. This is less confusing for Bob and makes game time more fun.

This family adapted a game for their son by changing the rules to fit Bob's way of learning and level of understanding. To eliminate confusion, everyone who was involved in the game used the same rules. The more concrete the rules can be, the better an autistic person will be able to participate.

USING STRUCTURE
Sometimes children can develop a social or leisure skill if the parents assist by providing more structure to help the child understand what is expected of him or her.

Since most autistic children learn best in structured situations (Schopler, Brehm, Kinsbourne, & Reichler, 1971), one of the first considerations for having a child learn how to occupy play and leisure time is to set aside a place specifically for that purpose. Areas that are not too large and have some definable boundaries help suggest to a child what can and cannot be done there. One mother and grandmother used an "area" to teach appropriate leisure skills, and they solved a destructive behavior problem at the same time.

At age 3½, Jack liked to leaf through magazines and books, which resulted in everything being torn up. We put away everything of value and fixed him a reading corner with a chair and old catalogs and magazines. These were his to play with whenever he wanted to, and as a result he left the other books alone. His grandmother also arranged a reading corner so that he could be occupied and happy when he visited Grandma, too.

Having a reading "area" helped Jack to settle in one place so that adults would not constantly have to be watching his movements. It conveyed to him that this was where he could play with books and magazines. Having his own catalogs and magazines let him do something he enjoyed while he learned to do it right (careful page turning), and this saved other reading materials from being destroyed by his interest in them. This parent focused on the child's interest in books and decided to build on that interest rather than emphasize his destructive behavior.

Autistic children will often spend unstructured free time in self-stimulation or games of chase, which can become behavior problems. One mother captured the dilemma that many parents face when their children are expected to occupy time on their own:

My 8-year-old son, Mario, is in a class in public school. The school insists that special children be "normal" and do what the other children in the school do. This includes three 20-minute recesses a day. The recesses were completely unstructured times during which the children were left to their own devices—a very stressful situation for my son. He paced up and down beside the playground fences and would sometimes sift leaves or grass through his fingers. I explained to the teacher that my son cannot come up with play ideas on his own. She now has some play materials (such as balls and ropes) available for him and lets him choose something to play with before each recess. (We taught him at home what to do with balls and ropes.) Even though he doesn't initiate play with other children yet, recess is not as stressful for my son now.

Because the classroom teacher did not provide activities or training during recess times, Mario often became anxious. This could have been because he did not know how to occupy the time himself or could have resulted from his not knowing how to approach and join in the games or activities that other children were playing on their own. When the teacher provided Mario with materials and structured the time for him by telling him what to do, he played more appropriately. This also increased the likelihood that the other children would join him in play or would encourage him to join them. Usually, however, this takes some specific training of peers by the teacher (Mesibov, 1992).

Materials are an important consideration in providing interest and structure for children. New and unbroken toys and age-appropriate materials can facilitate interest in playing (Schlein, Wehman, & Kiernan, 1981) and invite other children to join in. Removing preferred toys while reinforcing use of other toys and introducing toys that are similar to preferred toys may increase the play repertoire of children who repeatedly play with the same one or two toys. Often children are motivated by toys that give feedback, such as a jack-in-the-box does when it springs up after being wound. In this case, the toy itself provides the structure and doesn't require the child to understand its symbolic meaning or develop any elaborate play schemes.

The National Society for Autistic Children (1980) reports in its handbook *How They Grow* that parents and teachers have found the following toys useful as play items for young autistic children:

- Containers, shovels, sieves for sand and water
- Record players, music boxes, toy instruments
- Rocking or spring horses
- Books
- Jigsaw puzzles
- Shape discrimination toys
- Pegboards
- Pinwheels and spinning toys
- Construction toys like Legos™
- Toys that make noise
- Balls, especially large ones
- Large cartons such as a refrigerator box with soft material inside
- Chalkboards, tracing materials, beads for stringing, sewing cards, coloring and sticker books

Finding items that can hold a child's interest without triggering too many odd or stigmatizing behaviors is not always easy. Here is one success story:

> At times Jimmy, who's 3½, is very hyperactive and destructive. There are not many activities or toys that will sustain his interest and keep him occupied appropriately. We finally found that a hole dug in the backyard with soft dirt hills around it, a toy truck, a car, old spoons, and containers would keep him occupied for hours.

Jimmy's parents were able to find materials that motivated him to keep busy. These materials held his interest for long periods of time and were not inappropriate for a child his age to play with.

Some researchers (Favell, 1973; Hopper & Wambold, 1978) have found that prompting toy play and providing reinforcement (praise and food) increased interest in toy play and decreased stereotypies. Reinforcers that follow performance are often used in any area of learning to build motivation and reward increased skill performance, but motivation and skill performance frequently are enhanced by reinforcers built directly into the activity as these parents have done.

Another family found their vacation less enjoyable because of their worries about their son's safety until they helped structure the situation:

> Our family has a summer house on a lake. Our 10-year-old autistic son, Karl, cannot swim but is very active and enjoys playing in the water. In the past, we always worried about his safety and felt we had to keep a constant vigil. Then we thought of a simple safety device. We measured the distance from our lakeside chairs to the point in the water where he could play safely—that is, not get in over his head. My husband got two weighted posts and stretched a rope strung with colorful floats from my lakeside chair to the weighted post in the water, then stretched the rope to another weighted post across from the first, and back up to my husband's chair across from mine. Now my son stays in his "lifeguard" rope boundaries and can play in the water by himself while we watch from the beach.

These parents were not looking for a way to avoid having to keep an eye on Karl. They only wanted to be able to sit in one spot for a period of time rather than constantly chasing Karl or rescuing him from deep water. His parents were able to get some respite by coming up with a method that ensured his safety while allowing him more independence. The clear boundaries allowed him to control his own behavior.

Sometimes the structure can take the form of planned exercise routines. Daily exercise makes many people feel better. Relaxation and sleep come easier and are more restful. Most people try to make a conscious effort to undertake some type of activity every day, even if it is just a short walk.

One mother introduced exercise as a way of structuring some of her son's free time:

> My 16-year-old son, Tim, has a short attention span and can become hyperactive when not involved in some structured activity. This has presented problems at school and at home. He and I together have worked up to jogging 5 miles each morning. On days he exercises, his performance in school and his ability to occupy time at home are better than on days he does not exercise.

Tim's mother has found that exercise helps his school performance and prevents behavior problems that occur when he is in unstructured situations. He can concentrate for longer times and is more accepting of suggestions for activities during his free time. She has also discovered a leisure activity that she and her son can enjoy doing together. This activity could be expanded further to joining a local running club and entering local short-distance races. Also, Tim's mother is probably in terrific shape now!

Another mother shares a similar experience:

> My daughter Cindy, who is 10, is extremely hyperactive. We found that when she has nothing to do, she begins to get overactive. We taught her to use some of this energy by jumping on a trampoline or using a minijogger. This helps release the activity in a constructive manner. She also likes to run, and if we run with her twice a day it seems to calm her.

Cindy's activity level can intensify quickly to a disturbing level when she becomes excited. Burning off energy through appropriate physical leisure activities helps to calm Cindy. The activities her parents have chosen can be used throughout adolescence, too, because they are appropriate for any age.

Another parent found that this type of structure for her child's energy had the added dividend of protecting the furniture.

Jim, at 17, is somewhat hyperactive (but seems to be slowing down with time). After Jim trashed two couches by bouncing on them, I thought of purchasing a jogging trampoline. Jim just loves it. Although the trampoline only lasts about 1 year with Jim, it saves the furniture, keeps Jim in shape, and provides an outlet for energy as well as a leisure-time activity. Jim also realizes when he has a lot of energy to burn off and knows to go to the trampoline.

Adolescents often need an outlet for energy. Jim's parents have found the trampoline to be a necessary and useful piece of equipment (as many parents have stated). It helps him occupy free time appropriately, he enjoys it, it keeps him in shape, and it helps him control his own behavior by giving him a specific place and activity when he feels tense or anxious.

Research has also found that exercise decreases self-stimulation and can increase appropriate play and academic responding (Watters & Watters, 1980). Researchers have demonstrated that the type of exercise (mild versus vigorous) can affect hand flapping and other repetitive behaviors (Kern, Koegel, & Dunlap, 1984). They found that more vigorous and continuous (15 minutes) exercising such as jogging always reduced subsequent stereotypical behaviors when compared to an activity like playing ball.

As individuals get older, exercise becomes important for many job skills. Often jobs require a lot of standing, bending, lifting, and pulling. If stamina and strength are developed early, job placement and enjoyment can also be expected to be easier. One teacher has her students use the weight machines in the school gym a few days a week. This benefits their health and gives them an activity and skill enjoyed and respected by their nonhandicapped peers.

The parent handbook published by the National Society for Autistic Children (1980) lists the following outdoor equipment pieces as recommended by parents of autistic children: swings (ropes, tires, conventional), slides, wheel toys (wagons and tricycles), climbing towers and gym sets, trampolines and jumping boards, and revolving drums. As children get older and their skills advance, they may funnel energies into bike riding, skating, throwing a frisbee, or bowling.

BUILDING ON STRENGTHS

As parents know only too well, finding a leisure activity or an exercise for their child may sometimes be easier than motivating them to do it. The secret of success some parents have found is building on the child's own interests or strengths.

Sometimes exercise is needed for relaxation of muscle tightness caused by either medication, anxiety, or nervousness.

> When our son Dean was 15, some of his medication was causing a lot of muscle tightness. To combat this, we tried teaching him exercise routines and physical games. He didn't seem to enjoy these or want to participate, so they had little effect on his muscle tightness. Finally, we decided it would be better to pick a physical activity that he could already do and enjoyed, instead of teaching him something new. For Dean, this was bike riding. He enjoyed it, it relaxed him, and it had the desired effect on his muscle tightness.

Dean's parents knew that exercise would probably lessen his debilitating muscle tenseness. To make the exercise situation less frustrating, they used a physical activity that he already showed some skill in doing. This activity was then built up to a time period that had the effect of relaxing Dean's muscles.

Outdoor exercise circuits are springing up in many local communities. These can provide the place and motivation for an exercise routine and workout.

> My 12-year-old is very compulsive and loves routines. Karl was drawn to the structure of our local Vita Course. This particular course has 10 different exercise stations located at intervals along a 1½-mile path. Examples of the exercises are arm swings, toe touches, bar spring, and arm walk. Karl jogs between the stations and then does the exercise pictured at the station. Because it is very structured and routine, he does not need further motivators once he gets started. Karl has also made some friends with the regular course participants. They greet him as he passes them or they pass him.

Instead of having to plan for daily exercise for their child, this family made use of a community resource. Everything necessary for a workout was already in place. The routine layout of the exercise course was motivating to Karl, and so he did not have to be forced to exercise. He is also building a leisure skill that other persons can enjoy with him.

The Vita Course sounds like a good way of motivating some children to exercise. But the exercises may need to be taught and reviewed individually with autistic individuals before setting out on the course. A parent or teacher may want to number the exercises and draw numbered pictures of them for the child to carry on the course, similar to what this teacher did in her classroom:

> Each morning my adolescent students and I do an exercise routine. At first everyone was confused by the names of the exercises and the order in which they would be done. Now I have pictures of the starting position for each exercise, and the pictures are in the order the exercises are done, which can vary each day. This gives the students a visual way of realizing what exercise is coming next.

This teacher realized the importance of keeping up student participation in the daily exercise routine by making it understandable to them. Numbered pictures or simple drawings relieved student anxiety about what to do for each exercise and in what order to do the exercises. The students can now participate with less anxiety and greater pleasure because their task is comprehensible to them even though the order of exercises may change from day to day. Because the students liked routines, they enjoyed learning the exercises once they understood what was expected of them.

Sometimes a routine alone is not enough to motivate children to participate. The teacher in the following anecdote decided to cash in on her student's somewhat perseverative interest, turning it from a weakness into a strength.

> Niko, an overweight 11-year-old in my class, is preoccupied with geometric shapes. It was difficult to get him involved in any gross-motor activity. Finally, because of his interest in shapes, I got Niko to jog the triangular and square patterns made by the school's sidewalks. He now runs every day.

It is sometimes difficult to motivate overweight children into an activity beneficial to their health such as running. This teacher built on the child's own interest in shapes so that she could motivate him to exercise. He enjoys the activity while doing something beneficial for his health.

Even when a game is briefly enjoyed, some children soon get bored and lose interest. This mother found a way to increase her son's attention and interest in a game of ping-pong.

> I wanted to teach my 12-year-old son, Neil, an interactive game. Neil had shown skill at ping-pong. However, he did not understand keeping score, so he would get bored and begin to play inappropriately (hitting the ball off the ceiling, and so on). To get him to maintain appropriate play, he and I began to count the number of consecutive times we hit the ball to one another correctly instead of keeping score, which was too complex at this point for him. Neil was motivated to keep the count going as long as possible.

Neil understood the concept of playing toward a higher number of correctly hit balls and found that very exciting. His father adapted the game to Neil's level (since Neil did not understand conventional scorekeeping). He also built on Neil's love of numbers and counting to keep him motivated to hit the ball better and longer. Again, the parent built on the child's own interests and strengths as well as his current level of understanding.

Overweight and with a dislike for physical activity, Andy presented a double challenge to his mother. She found a way to motivate him to run laps from his house to the mailbox.

> My 15-year-old son, Andy, is not physically active and consequently has become overweight. My problem was that I could not get him to exercise. He is very interested in television and magazines and gets especially excited by the numerical scores used in reporting on sports. I measured the distance between the mailbox and the house and multiplied this to get how many laps would equal 1 mile. Then I stocked the refrigerator with low-calorie foods. My son now enjoys running, counting miles run per day, counting calories, and talking about sports records.

This mother knew that telling Andy that he must run or that he had to eat certain foods would probably have been met with resistance.

Instead, she made the activities fit his interests and built the reinforcing element—his preoccupation with numbers—into the activities.

Another important reason for teaching play and leisure activities is to build skills that children can use during times when adults cannot be directly involved with them. Parents also have to tend to other family responsibilities, as well as needing time for themselves apart from their children.

One mother enjoys doing the following free-time activity with her child, but it is also something that the daughter could potentially do on her own while her mother relaxed or worked on a project of her own.

Cathy, age 11, enjoys reading and writing at school but can't always find something to do on her own at home. So I ordered *Weekly Reader* on an elementary level for her to read during free time at home. Sometimes we work on it together. It has easy to read stories, puzzles, and other things that help her build academic skills. It's different enough from what she does at school that she is not bored with it. There are enough activities in one *Weekly Reader* issue to keep her busy for two to three 20-minute periods.

Because this activity is one that Cathy can do without a lot of parent intervention, it is not different from what parents might use to help a nonhandicapped child occupy free time. By providing the structure of a guided reading program, this mother encouraged her daughter to spend leisure time appropriately. The mother can complete other tasks while Cathy is occupied.

Here is another example of a child who needed a suggestion from parents to help occupy free time more constructively:

Our 13-year-old son has many of the same interests as a nonhandicapped teenager. Jerry can sit and listen to rock music for long periods of time. To make that leisure time a bit more purposeful, we suggested to him that he draw pictures while listening to his music. He surprised us by winning first place in his school's talent contest. He illustrated and accompanied one of his favorite songs with abstract drawings done on Kodak's Ektagraphic write-on slides.

Jerry already occupied free time age-appropriately with his rock music, but his parents wanted to add some variety to that time, so they suggested drawing. There are many simple arts and crafts activities that children can do independently once they have been guided through the basic steps successfully. By paying attention to Jerry's strong interest in music and following his lead, these parents were able to discover a real talent that is the envy of many a family of nonhandicapped adolescent rock listeners.

DEVELOPING SOCIALIZATION AND COMMUNITY INTEGRATION

Interactions with Peers

Once play and leisure skills are developed, they may be used to encourage siblings and neighborhood children to interact more freely with the handicapped child. The autistic child will probably still need assistance and reinforcement, but often successful interactions with other children will serve as a motivator for more interactions and development of better skills.

The family in the following anecdote used an already developed play skill to bring together their child and some neighborhood children.

> Eugene, our 11-year-old, is a furniture bouncer. We have successfully transferred this skill to a jogging trampoline. Usually his trampoline is kept in the basement so that he can bounce out of the way of obstacles. But during the summer months, the bouncer goes out onto the porch where neighborhood children also take turns jumping.

Usually autistic children are on the fringe of a group that is playing, because they do not have the play skills necessary to join in. In this situation, the autistic child is the one who is skilled in trampoline jumping. The other children are interested in doing it with him. Initially, an adult might have to provide some structure while the neighbor children are there, organizing the order and length of turns so that the autistic child realizes that his or her turn will come again. It should not be difficult for the neighborhood children to then begin structuring turns for the autistic child.

Another family used interest in interacting with neighborhood children to further develop play skills:

When our 9-year-old daughter, Tina, sees the neighborhood children, she wants to play with them but can't keep up with groups. So I invite the child who shows the most interest in playing with her. In this way our daughter can learn and play the same games as the other children but in a situation that is much easier for her to handle. For example, she won't participate when a group of children is roller skating on the sidewalks, but she and a friend enjoy practicing skating in the garage with music from the record player.

In both of the preceding examples, parents were successful at building interactive play skills because they used something that their child was already successful at doing or was very interested in, such as trampoline jumping or wanting to interact with neighbor children. They also found other children who shared their child's interest. Teachers, too, have realized that once some play or leisure skills have been taught individually, introducing normal peers as playmates can facilitate teaching and learning of cooperative play and socialization skills. This teacher of primary-age students used this fact well:

It was difficult to mainstream my students into a regular physical education (PE) class. With all the students and the activities, they would get intimidated and do a lot of hand flapping and noise making. I decided that they would do better if they learned the routines first in a less confusing setting. I had six students from the fourth grade come to my room for PE. This gave my students good peer models in a controlled atmosphere. It helped the children from regular education better understand the autistic children and helped the autistic children learn to function in a larger group. We played group and table games and danced. Now my students look forward to going to "regular" PE, pairing up with their "buddies" and doing what the other kids do. If one of my kids gets confused or distracted, he has a pal who knows how to help him get back on track.

This teacher realized that children are the experts on playing, so she used them as examples and teachers for training play skills while an adult provided the structure and direction. Another teacher, who also incorporated play groups with normal peers into her classroom, prepared the peers for interacting with the autistic students by giving them a booklet. The booklet told how the students with autism are the same as and different from normal peers. She also listed tips on how to play with autistic children, such as "You may have to be bossy sometimes."

Access to Community Recreation and Leisure Facilities

Another avenue for play and leisure with normal peers is through local Parks and Recreation programs.

Each time I took my nonhandicapped son, Joe, for swimming lessons, his sister, Eileen, would whine and cry to join them. I spent the whole time holding her back or walking with her around and around the recreation area until my son's lesson was over. One day Eileen escaped my grasp and jumped into the shallow pool. Chagrined, I went into the pool and had to drag her out while she kicked and screamed. The second time it happened, the instructor turned to me and told me to get her out. Looking at her paddling happily in the water, I said, "If you want to get her out, you'll have to do it yourself." Remembering our previous scene, he let her be. Either the sight of the usually whining child transformed into the happy paddler or the knowledge that he was going to have to be the "heavy" convinced him to talk to the recreation director. Now Eileen is taking swimming lessons too.

This mother finally tired of her role in supporting the Recreation Department's exclusion of children with handicaps. Fortunately, in this case, the child was not endangered by her plunge as many other children might have been. As this mother came to realize, parents of children with disabilities are entitled to community recreation programs. Most communities now recognize this. Unfortunately, community programs are sometimes not used because parents of children with special needs are not aware of them. If parents discover that an appropriate program is not available through their recreation department, they may want to offer some assistance in setting up something in their area.

Other community leisure opportunities can also provide pleasurable experiences for autistic individuals. As the following anecdote illustrates, it is true that both leisure skills and behaviors are best taught in natural settings.

A few weeks ago, we took Carlos (age 5) along when his sister was going roller skating at the local rink. I did not think that he would be able to skate or that he would enjoy anything about the roller rink, and I expected to have to deal with a lot of crying and chasing. Instead, he accepted putting on skates, and after much encouragement and praise, he was able to go around the rink holding the railing and my hand. He had great fun and seemed so proud of himself. We are now going to try other community experiences like the library and the swimming pool.

Although his mother was skeptical as to how Carlos would handle roller skating, it turned into a delightful experience. If he continues to show interest in roller skating and is given opportunities to visit the rink, he will have developed a community-based leisure skill by the time he is an adolescent.

Vacations can be another area of family concern. Parents have pointed out that sometimes it helps first to rent a vacation place where the family has more privacy from other vacationers—a cabin or beach house—and then to try a more crowded setting like a motel. Other parents advised taking along some of the child's favorite possessions. Some parents explain to the child how a vacation works by showing pictures of where they will stay and by putting the pictures in order of events (car, mountains, cabin, car, home).

Although the need for solutions to play and leisure problems may not seem as pressing as problems of aggression or self-help skills, the lack of skills in this area can effectively exclude children from participation in their neighborhood and community. The examples and stories in the preceding pages demonstrate that parents and teachers can be creative in problem solving and are aware of how to use childrens' interests and abilities effectively to promote growth in the play and leisure area.

REFERENCES

American Psychiatric Association. (1994). *Diagnostic and Statistical Manual of Mental Disorders* (4th ed.). Washington, DC: Author.

Favell, J. (1973). Reduction of stereotypies by reinforcement of toy play. *Mental Retardation, 11 (4)*, 21–23.

Hopper, C., & Wambold, C. (1978, February). Improving the independent play of severely mentally retarded children. *Education and Training of the Mentally Retarded,* pp. 42–46.

Kern, L., Koegel, R., & Dunlap, G. (1984). The influence of vigorous versus mild exercise on autistic stereotyped behaviors. *Journal of Autism and Developmental Disorders, 10* (4), 379–387.

Mesibov, G. B. (1992). Treatment issues with high functioning adolescents and adults with autism. In E. Schopler & G. B. Mesibov (Eds.), *High Functioning Individuals with Autism* (pp. 143–155). New York: Plenum Press.

National Society for Autistic Children. (1977, July). *Definition of the syndrome of autism.* Approved by the Board of Directors and the Professional Advisory Board.

National Society for Autistic Children. (1980). *How they grow: A handbook for parents of young children with autism.* Washington, DC: Author.

Schlein, S., Wehman, P., & Kiernan, J. (1981). Teaching leisure skills to severely handicapped adults: An age-appropriate darts game. *Journal of Applied Behavior Analysis, 14* (4), 513–519.

Schopler, E., Brehm, S., Kinsbourne, M., & Reichler, R. (1971). Effect of treatment structure on development in autistic children. *Archives of General Psychiatry, 24,* 415–421.

Watters, R., & Watters, W. (1980). Decreasing self-stimulatory behavior with physical exercise in a group of autistic boys. *Journal of Autism and Developmental Disorders, 10* (4), 379–387.

5

Aggression

**Problem
Behaviors**

**Underlying
Deficits**

A lmost nothing causes as much distress to parents as their autistic child's aggressive behavior. Although it is a serious problem in only a small percentage of autistic children and adolescents, when it occurs, pushing, hitting, spitting, throwing, or destroying property may endanger the child and his or her family, or at least seriously disrupt normal family life. Aggressive behavior usually is not life threatening, but may be the "final straw" that overwhelms the family or causes the autistic person to be ejected from his or her classroom, workshop, or group home. Because of its importance, both parents and professionals have put considerable creative energy into understanding and solving problems of aggression.

The tip of the iceberg (see the iceberg analogy in Chapter 1) or the aggressive behaviors such as hitting, banging, or biting are obvious. Sometimes, however, the underlying deficits that trigger the behaviors are not so obvious. Frustration over communication problems, poor social judgment, lack of awareness of self and others, and sensory misperceptions can all contribute to the problem. Both parents and professionals (Mulick & Durand, 1989) have proposed solutions that deal with underlying deficits as well as with the aggressive behaviors themselves.

In the sections that follow, we share both parental and professional solutions to three types of aggressive behavior: aggression against the self, or self-injury; aggression against other people; and aggression against or destruction of property. Remember, we are not proposing any solution as a panacea for all problems or all children. What works for one child in one setting may not work for another child or in another setting. Certainly if a behavior that could result in injury to the child or his or her family does not respond to home remedies, professional help should be enlisted.

AGGRESSION AGAINST SELF, OR SELF-INJURY

Watching someone hurt your child accidentally is a difficult experience for parents. Watching your child deliberately injure himself or herself is almost intolerable. Most autistic children do not inflict physical injury on themselves, but for those who do, it is a serious and stressful problem for families.

Head Banging

This section contains solutions found for children who banged their heads against windows or other objects or who hit their head or some part of it (e.g., eyes) with their hands or objects.

This parent tells of her child who abruptly started banging her head with her hand:

> After two ear infections, Jane would hit her head with her hand. We tried positive reinforcement, negative reinforcement, and restraints. She was still a very unhappy little girl, and with elbow restraints she would move to hitting her thighs. Finally, we found a way to stop her head banging using spinning activities. Four hours a day were spent in spinning play and on merry-go-rounds and tire swings that moved in circles. Within 4 weeks she had quit head banging. The time spent on the playground was slowly decreased to outside play with other children for two half-hour periods.

After trying a variety of solutions, this parent and teacher capitalized on Jane's enjoyment of spinning objects and spinning activities to stop the head banging. Although there are research reports of using similar activities to stop self-injury (MacLean & Baumeister, 1982), it may or may not have been the spinning that was responsible for stopping the head banging. Apart from the spinning, Jane was receiving a great deal of attention for behaviors that were incompatible with head banging. (It's difficult to both bang your head and hold onto a swing or merry-go-round!)

Jane's parents also saw a connection between the child's head banging and her recurrent ear infections. The assumption that there is a connection between the two is supported by research with nonhandicapped children (Cataldo & Harris, 1982). This research shows that some cases of head banging begin with ear infections, although in normal children the head banging usually stops without any special intervention. Knowing about the possible link between ear infections and head banging, other parents also reported checking for physical ailments that might require medical care when there was a sudden onset of head banging or other unusual behaviors. (See also the discussion on aggression against others later in this chapter.) Parents noted that this was especially important when they had nonverbal children who had no other way of letting them know that they were in pain.

A different approach to stopping head banging worked for another child:

> My son Michael, age 7, who is a head banger, is in a special education class in public school. The school insisted that his class be "normal"— that is, do what the other classes in the school do. This included three 20-minute recesses a day. The recesses were completely unstructured times during which the children were left to their own devices. My son spent the time hand flapping and head banging. Not only did this not help to make him any more "normal," but other kids who saw him doing this thought he was weird and stayed away from him. We insisted that the school provide some structured play activities for him during recess periods. He stopped flapping and head banging and looked a lot more normal.

These parents wisely recognized that their son's head banging was more likely to occur when the child was bored or had nothing to do. They also realized that this attempt to provide an unstructured "normal" play situation for their child resulted in his behaving in a way that was unlikely to encourage other children to play with him. The parents also had a good working relationship with the teacher and were able to observe the child, identify a need, and bring about changes in the child's program.

Professionals have also found that self-injury is least apt to occur in school settings where the child is involved in an activity and closely supervised by the teacher (MacLean & Baumeister, 1982). Particularly with lower functioning autistic children, a structured school environment is generally most effective. Another study (Berkson & Mason, 1964) showed that head banging, rocking, and hand movements of retarded persons occurred more frequently in a bare room than in a similar room in which a rubber ball, a plastic train, and a furry toy dog were available. Having something to do cut down on the head banging and other inappropriate behaviors. In this instance, Michael's parents helped guide the school into providing appropriate, structured play activities for their child. Without parental input in this case, apparent "normalization" may have inadvertently placed this autistic child in a situation that actually increased self-injurious behavior.

One head banger "worked" nights:

> My son Matthew is an on-again off-again head banger. He likes the security of bed sheets tucking him tightly in bed and the feel of the blankets next to his skin. He also likes to roll around in bed, which created a problem. Whenever he rolled, he pulled the blankets out; then when he was uncovered, he would bang his head on his headboard. I solved the problem by making summer and winter "sacks." I folded a blanket, sewing the bottom and stitching the sides together, and putting in a zipper and elastic around the top (creating a center opening sleeping bag). I sewed a sheet and a blanket together for a winter sack. Now nights are no problem—my son loves his sack!

This parent knew that Matthew liked to be tucked in tightly, and she adjusted his bedding to meet both this preference and his tendency to roll around in bed. Whether Matthew liked the reassurance of being confined in the sack or the tactile sensation of the fabric, or simply staying warm all night, the solution worked. For some parents without sewing skills or time, a lightweight sleeping bag might serve the same purpose.

Another parent believed that she got her son to quit head banging by helping him to understand the consequences of head banging:

> We were having a terrible time with my 5-year-old son, Eddie, when he started public school. He would start banging his head every time he didn't get his way. The head banging would cause a problem on the school bus, in school, or at home. I tried to tell him that this would hurt him, but he didn't seem to have any sense of the damage he could do. One day when he was at home and started banging his head on the table, I took an egg and put it in a dish. I told Eddie to bang the egg "like you bang your head." He banged the egg on the dish and it

smashed into a thousand pieces. When the egg broke, he stopped and stared at it. I told him that's what can happen to your head. He never banged his head after that.

This parent decided to find a graphic way that the child would understand to illustrate her repeated warnings on the dangers of head banging. Again, it is not possible to say whether the egg story and the end to the head banging were a fortunate coincidence or whether Eddie really did understand better. This same solution might be ineffective or frightening for another child, but the idea of finding concrete ways to communicate with the child on his or her own level is an important part of solving most problems. Many parents have observed that their young, autistic children do not seem to have any real notion of the danger of self-injury. Some autistic children have a reduced sensitivity to the pain that would ordinarily set limits on head banging in nonhandicapped children.

Sometimes children bang their heads against objects, as this mother points out:

Our daughter Shari banged her head on her window in her bedroom and also tore down any curtains or drapes we put up, breaking metal rods and tearing hardware out of the wall. To solve this problem, we mounted Venetian-type blinds inside the casing with a sheet of plexiglass attached to the casings on the side facing the bedroom. There are small holes cut in the plexiglass for ventilation, for opening the window, and for raising and opening the blinds. Not only was the plexiglass less dangerous, but it didn't make a loud noise when Shari banged on it. Banging it didn't get such a rise out of me, so Shari soon stopped banging.

Shari's mother, faced with both the possibility of serious injury for her child and the cost of replacing drapes and rods, eliminated both head banging and drapery destruction by changing the environment. By installing the plexiglass shield, these parents eliminated the danger and the damage. As her mother notes, Shari's banging the plexiglass did not pay off either in noise or in attention from her parents as glass banging had. Knowing the child was safe, the parents could ignore the banging and not inadvertently reinforce this destructive behavior.

Eye Poking

Some autistic persons actually seem to seek pain or stimulation. One researcher describes how this information was used to design a solution (Favell, McGimsey, & Schnell, 1982):

> Jeff was a profoundly mentally retarded 22-year-old who had limited vision. He would routinely press his finger against his open eye. School staff had tried to control the behavior by physically interrupting Jeff when he did it and by planning lots of activities for him, but the behavior continued. Experimenters found that when bright, visual toys such as prisms, mirrors, and shiny toys were made available to him, eye poking decreased. Jeff needed special instruction, however, to learn to play with the toys instead of just spinning or flicking them.

In this case, it appears that finding a more appropriate way to provide visual stimulation through toys stopped the eye poking. Other researchers (Wells & Smith, 1983) used a similar approach. By applying a vibrator to the child's hand, self-injury with hands dropped dramatically. By taking the child's perspective, it is sometimes possible to figure out what payoff the behavior has for the child and to find more appropriate ways to provide the stimulation.

Self-Biting

Sometimes self-biting or other self-injurious behaviors occur in situations where someone is making some demand on the child.

> My son Ben would bite his hand whenever I tried to get him to do something like dress himself or stop watching TV and get ready for bed. For a while, he had me buffaloed and I would back off and let him have his way so that he didn't hurt himself. Finally I decided that he couldn't go through life without doing some things he didn't like. At first when I forced him to turn off the TV or get dressed, his biting increased, and I thought I would have to give up. Instead I made him do what he was supposed to, and I sang one of his favorite songs to distract us from the biting. He's pretty stubborn, but so am I. When he figured out I meant business and he'd have to get dressed anyway, he stopped biting his hand. Sometimes he still wants me to sing while he gets dressed.

This mother figured out that if a child can escape demands by engaging in self-injurious behavior, he or she will. Ben's mother decided to ignore the biting and to eliminate the escape from reasonable demands that it provided. She also paired singing, one of Ben's favorite activities, with going through the motions (at first forced) of getting dressed or whatever the appropriate activity was. This reinforced behavior that was incompatible with biting. (It's hard to bite your hand and put your arm through a sleeve at the same time.)

A different strategy solved Duncan's biting problem:

> My 7-year-old son, Duncan, had been doing very well in school, behaving himself and even making some slow but significant gains in simple signs and self-help skills. His teacher told me that she had great expectations for him. Not long afterward, Duncan started biting his knuckles until they bled at school, but he didn't bite them at home. I went to school and observed Duncan in his classroom. Duncan, who knew just a few simple signs, was being communicated with and being asked to communicate in extremely rapid and complex signing by a student teacher assigned to his class. Enthused by his initial progress, the student teacher had Duncan in over his head in a signing program that was simply too difficult for him. I talked to the teacher and student teacher, and they agreed to back up to a signing level where Duncan could be successful. When they did, the knuckle biting stopped. The teacher gradually increased the difficulty of the program, being careful to challenge Duncan but not to overwhelm him.

Duncan's mother recognized that the biting was his response to a program that was not appropriate for his level. When classroom demands were at a level that Duncan could respond to, his frustration disappeared and his biting stopped. In Ben's case above, self-biting served as an escape from reasonable demands that he could handle. The objective there was to get him to do what was reasonable. In this case, it would not be reasonable (or even possible) to force Duncan to do more than he was capable of. Solving these biting problems that at first look very similar requires knowledge of the child, his current developmental level, and the demands being made on him.

One mother sensed that her response to her child's self-biting was somehow a payoff for him.

> My 3-year-old son Greg's self-abusive behavior involved biting his wrist until it bled. It caused me great pain to see this behavior, and no matter

how I tried to mask my upset, Greg knew it bothered me. I could not ignore the behavior, and I could not stop it. In desperation, I brought a piece of saddle leather and cut an egg shape with a hole for his thumb. I then attached the leather to a knit ribbing cuff. Next I sewed a small dog collar to buckle around the wrist so that the protective device could not be removed. No matter how hard Greg bit it, it gave him no satisfaction—no pain and no attention. When I knew he was not hurting or scarring himself, I could ignore the behavior. In a month the behavior was only random. The wrist protection could be removed for longer and longer periods of time and finally discarded altogether. A year later there was no more wrist biting.

This parent knew she could ignore her child's biting only if she was certain the child was safe from danger. Making the protective device eliminated both the sensory stimulation the child was receiving from biting and the attention he invariably got from his mother who was upset about the biting. Greg's mother also found ways to give him attention when he was engaged in appropriate behavior like playing with toys. The biting, then, at least helped communicate to Greg's mother that her attention was important to him.

The child's inability to express his needs and frustrations may also result in the child's biting himself or others.

When Ian was picked on by the other kids in his class, he would get very upset and start to bite his arm, often to the point of tearing the skin and causing it to bleed. When his teacher realized that the biting seemed to happen after these episodes, she taught Ian a more appropriate way to communicate his distress. When he learned to shout "Knock it off" to the classmates who were tormenting him, the self-biting dropped off almost entirely.

Ian's biting was in response to his frustration in not being able to communicate. This teacher helped Ian find an appropriate way to communicate his distress; she gave him a directive that was age-appropriate and easily understood by his classmates. In this case, having an alternative way to express his frustration eliminated Ian's self-biting. In most cases, however, just teaching communication skills alone is not enough to eliminate the self-injurious behavior. The example should serve to illustrate, though, how an underlying deficit may need to be addressed as well as the more obvious "tip of the iceberg" behavior. Schroeder, Schroeder, Rojahn, and Mulick (1981) point out that for the severely retarded person without communication skills, self-injurious behavior, which cannot be ignored, can be tantamount to establishing communication and some control of the environment.

Hair Pulling

One self-injurious behavior, hair pulling, was handled successfully by these parents:

> Our 16-year-old son, Mark, suddenly began pulling out his hair. We put Vaseline in his hair, so that when he went to pull it out, his fingers just slid through. (His spiky hair made him look a little "punk," but we thought that was less conspicuous than a bald spot would be!) We had to do this daily for approximately 1 week before he stopped pulling his hair out. We think we nipped this odd behavior in the bud before it got to be a long-standing habit.

This solution allowed the parents to ignore the behavior and also reduced the sensory stimulation "payoff" Mark got from pulling his hair. Because the parents acted quickly and effectively, they prevented their son from developing a disturbing and conspicuous habit.

Knuckle Squeezing

Sometimes self-injurious behaviors may actually cause medical problems if left untreated:

> Our son Matthew would squeeze the knuckles of his left hand so hard that the doctor was concerned about problems with arthritis in that hand. We tried ignoring, scolding, and punishing him, but nothing made him stop. Finally, we put a thickly padded glove securely on his left hand, leaving his dominant right hand free to use in other activities. Matthew earned increasing periods of time with the glove off by not squeezing his knuckles. When the behavior was safely stopped for a long period of time, we took off the glove. He almost never squeezes his knuckles anymore. If on a rare occasion he forgets, just taking the glove out is enough to get him to stop.

Matthew's parents prevented him from getting any reinforcing stimulation by having him wear a glove on the hand he squeezed.

Presumably, they also provided activities for Matthew that kept his right hand busy and distracted him from the hand squeezing. It is clear that the glove became a discriminant stimulus, or signal for Matthew, since just the appearance of the glove could eventually get him to stop knuckle squeezing.

Window Banging

Some behaviors you cannot just ignore, but must stop from occurring. A number of parents did this, not by changing the behavior, but by changing the environment so that the problem could not occur. This approach is particularly necessary for behaviors so dangerous that one occurrence could cause serious injury:

> Our 12-year-old daughter Lucy would jump out of the second-story windows in our house. We tried all kinds of locks, but she loved to play with locks and figured out how to unlock them. We also tried chicken wire over the windows, but she would pull it down and could get cut on it. Anything "extra" on the window just seemed to draw her attention to it more. Finally, on our windows, which had wooden frames with half-circle locks, we put a screw in the frame in front of the lock where the thumb manipulates the lock. This way, a screwdriver was needed to remove the screw and open the window. The screw wasn't attractive and shiny like locks were, so she left it alone and finally gave up trying to open the windows and jump out.

Since Lucy was attracted to any additional paraphernalia on the window, the parents' original attempts to seal the window with special locks or chicken wire were ineffective. A common screw in an effective but inconspicuous place provided the protection and discouragement their daughter needed.

The above solution worked for Lucy, but it wouldn't be effective for Audrey, who also climbed out of windows. Her exit was made not by opening the window, but by breaking the glass with a toy or other object or even with her hands.

> We tried everything to keep Audrey away from her windows, but we couldn't leave her in her bedroom without her trying to bash through the window with a shoe, a toy, or one day even her fist. We had to protect her

and the window. We used metal grates that are normally used for screen doors to cover the inside frame of the window. This way we can still open the window for air (by using a pole through the holes in the grate), but Audrey can't get hurt breaking the glass or climbing out the window.

A child who was somewhat less persistent than Audrey was stopped with a similar approach:

Erin was a window banger. We were very afraid he would hurt himself on broken glass. To save our sanity and Erin's health, we placed shutters on the lower half of the windows so that he couldn't bang the glass. This worked for a while. When Erin learned how to open shutters, we made a screen for the inside of his window. We took screening the size of our window frames, stapled the screening to a frame my husband made out of inexpensive wood molding, and painted the molding frame to match the inside window frame. We then attached the frame with small screws to the inside window frame. Unless you looked very closely, you could not tell the screen was on the wrong side of the window. Light continued to stream into our rooms, and Erin was safe because when he tried to bang, he hit the screening and not the glass. After Erin outgrew his window-pounding stage, it was a simple matter to remove the screening, fill the four screw holes, and touch it up with a dab of paint.

These parents found a solution to the window-banging problem that maintained the normal appearance of the child's room. Little effort was needed to return the window to its original status once the child outgrew the window-banging habit.

Nose Peeling

Another parent had a daughter whose nose peeling was a serious problem:

Our 6-year-old daughter, Allison, would peel the skin off her nose so that it was bleeding constantly. We tried scolding, getting her involved in other activities that used her hands, and ignoring the behavior. Nothing worked, and scarring was becoming a problem. Finally we made a cardboard device that slipped on both arms and prevented her from bending her arms at the elbows to reach her nose. She even slept in the restraints because nighttime was a particularly bad time for picking and bleeding. Her hands were still free to do other things. In 6 weeks, we gradually reduced the amount of time she wore the cardboard restraints, then put them on only after a skin-peeling episode. Allison stopped skin peeling, and the cardboard restraints were no longer needed.

Only by preventing Allison from being able to reach her nose could these parents prevent her from peeling her nose. They were careful to see that Allison's hands were free and her schedule was filled with activities that interested her and required her to use her hands. In this way, they reinforced her use of her hands for appropriate activities that would compete with nose peeling. By gradually reducing the time Allison wore the restraints, the parents were able to eventually get rid of both the bad habit and the restraints.

There have also been many professional accounts of the successful use of restraints (Saposnek & Watson, 1974) and many earlier accounts of abuses of restraints where they were used habitually, not systematically and briefly to treat a behavior. Any procedure involving restraints should be carefully considered and discontinued if it is not working. In at least one case (Favell, McGimsey, & Jones, 1978), the procedure worked in reverse, with the retarded person refraining from self-injurious behavior in order to get to wear a restraint. What might stop the behavior for one child might actually reinforce it for another, so careful observation of the actual rather than the intended effect of any intervention is needed.

In reviewing parent and professional approaches to the problem of self-injury, a number of differences are apparent. Most of the accounts in the professional literature deal with self-injurious behavior that has persisted for years, usually with persons living in institutions. Many, if not most, of the cases described in the professional literature involve adults, and the successful interventions take place in controlled environments or laboratory settings. On the other hand, the successful parent solutions involve persons living at home, most of them children, and in many cases, the parents are stopping a relatively new behavior before it becomes a persistent habit. Because severe self-injury that has persisted over time is so difficult to eliminate, early parental interventions are particularly important.

Long-term self-injurious behavior may be one of the hardest problems for either parents or professionals to deal with effectively, and no single intervention or solution works for self-injurious behavior as opposed to other kinds of behaviors. Few parent or professional accounts report long-term follow-up on the success of the solutions, and few report whether stopping one behavior results in the development of a different self-injurious behavior. The parent efforts described here are most apt to be effective before the behavior becomes an established habit.

AGGRESSION AGAINST OTHERS

Hitting or Kicking Others

The autistic child's frustration over his or her inability to communicate may lead to pushing, biting, or spitting at brothers and sisters or other children in the neighborhood or at school. The following father's example illustrates this point:

> My 5-year-old daughter, Carol, was often frustrated, and she hit and kicked other people, including teachers and other children. At home we could understand what she wanted, but people outside the house could not. I persuaded the school to stop thinking Carol was deliberately being mean and to concentrate instead on helping her learn sign language so that she would have a more appropriate way to let people know what she wanted or needed. She learned 300 signs in 6 months, and her frustration level and aggression dropped dramatically at that point.

This father saw Carol's aggressive behavior as a response to the frustration of not being able to communicate. Instead of punishing her and increasing her frustration, he succeeded in working with the school to provide an appropriate, although nonverbal, way for her to be understood. The problem may be especially serious for nonverbal children until they learn some means to communicate their needs and feelings. No amount of punishment for the aggressive behavior will be sufficient if the child does not have an acceptable way to let people know what he or she needs or feels.

Other parents have also recognized that hitting and biting can be caused by communication deficits:

> When our daughter Mary, who had very little language, started screaming, biting, or hitting us, she was usually trying to tell us something. In

the past, we would ask her what she wanted. When she was unable to tell us, she would get more frustrated, her behavior would get worse, and my wife and I would get upset. Now when Mary starts to get upset, we have her sit down, and we ask her simple questions that require only a "yes" or "no" answer, such as "Do you have to potty?" "Is the belt too tight?" "Did you lose the pencil?" She doesn't have to give a complicated response; she just has to shake her head yes or no. Now she knows we're trying to understand her, and eventually we'll figure out what she needs. She calms right down. When kids are upset is no time for a long discussion.

This father saw his child's aggression as a primitive form of communication. Instead of escalating the problem for both the child and the parents by scolding or punishing, he focused on trying to understand what the child wanted. These parents avoided long discussions, simplified their own language, and structured the situation so that only a motor response was required from the child. This approach not only enabled Mary to communicate her needs, but it avoided escalating the friction between parents and child.

Another approach was suggested by a teacher of a high-functioning, autistic adolescent boy who liked to write.

When Allan gets angry, his parents or teachers tell him to sit down and write about how he feels. He now does this on his own. His parents find notes that say, "I want to punch Jimmy in the stomach," but after writing the note, he calms down and doesn't actually punch Jimmy. He's also learned that when he's really upset he can ask to go to the bathroom (or at home he can go to his room) to say mean things about someone he's angry with. He doesn't do this in public, and his behavior is much more acceptable to other kids now.

Because autistic children and adults often do not express their feelings appropriately, parents and teachers sometimes assume that they don't have feelings. This teacher found an appropriate way to have Allan express his feelings (in writing and in private) without having him act them out aggressively. The teacher was also aware that aggressive words and actions make an adolescent unpopular with others. Writing down his angry feelings reduced the number of times he actually hit others and also eliminated verbal tirades that would get him into difficulty.

Biting

The following parent stories regarding biting illustrate a number of other explanations for aggressive behavior.

My 8-year-old son, Mark, started biting people although he never had before. The school was ready to kick him out. I noticed that the other children in his class had already lost their baby teeth, but he hadn't yet. On checking, we found that he had five loose teeth that were causing him pain. His brothers at that age just pulled their teeth out when they got loose. He didn't know enough to do that, and he started biting in an effort to relieve the pain. Our dentist helped me remove the loose teeth over a 2-week period, and the biting problem ended.

An autistic child's inability to communicate may mask some underlying problem that is causing the child pain. The child may express this by acting out. Mark's mother was perceptive enough to link the sudden onset of biting with Mark's developmental schedule for getting new teeth. As in the example above regarding ear infections and head banging, the sudden onset of a behavior served as a signal to check first for some underlying physical cause. Another parent scheduled a dental checkup for a biting child and discovered that the child had cavities that were causing him pain. When the cavities were filled and the pain was gone, the biting stopped.

A different source of pain was identified by parents of another biting child:

My nonverbal son, Chris, started biting his brother and sister and other children at school. This was shortly after the doctor put him on Dilantin for seizures. We checked with the doctor to see if there could be any connection. He said that Dilantin can cause swelling and soreness in the gums. He advised us to rub Orajel (for teething pain for babies) on his gums. We did and the biting dropped dramatically.

Parents are not always informed of possible side effects of new medication. Fortunately Chris's mother checked with the doctor when her child began biting shortly after being put on antiseizure medication. The teething medication relieved the child's gum pain and stopped the biting. Although the link is not always so clear, reporting any unusual symptoms to the physician when your child is on medication can lead to changes in medication or to better control of side effects.

Some parents have found consistent, mild punishment effective.

> We tried everything to get my son Penn to stop biting people. Nothing worked. Finally, we told him, "People hate it when you bite them," and we put a blindfold on him for 30 seconds each time he bit someone. Whether doing something he hated helped him understand how other people felt when he did something they hated, I don't know, but it did stop the biting.

Penn's parents found that a consistently applied mild punishment, blindfolding for 30 seconds, stopped the biting. Whether he understood the quid pro quo is uncertain, but the solution worked for them in dealing with a serious, long-standing problem.

Other parents have not been successful in finding a specific cause for the biting, but have been successful in changing the target of the biting.

> When my son Tony was upset, he started biting other children. We gave him a rubber toy animal to bite when he was upset and taught him to bite the toy, not other people. The biting was especially problematic when his new second teeth were coming in, and the small rubber toy helped him through this period.

Tony's mother redirected the biting to a toy. Although biting a rubber toy may not be age-appropriate for a 6-year-old, it is more appropriate than biting people. Again, these parents were able to link biting with the emergence of their child's second teeth.

Pinching

A similar switch from person to object worked for a pinching problem.:

> My 14-year-old daughter, Eunice, would pinch people when she got upset. Her teacher gave her a beanbag to pinch, and now she'll pinch that instead of people.

The teacher redirected the child's aggression from persons to an object. Sometimes behaviors like pinching get such a response from the victims that the pincher is reinforced by all the attention and fuss. With the beanbag, no damage was done to anyone, and the child did not become the center of attention for pinching.

Many parents have indicated that their children are most apt to be aggressive—hitting, kicking, and biting—when they have a lot of pent-up energy. Robert's story illustrates this point.

> Robert, our 17-year-old son, is very physical. Hitting other people when he is upset is not acceptable. We put a punching bag in the corner of his room. When we see him getting upset, we direct him to the punching bag. Sometimes he even tells us he needs the punching bag. This has helped him deal more appropriately with his anger.

These parents have found it best to diffuse the situation as soon as they can see the child start to get very agitated and active. They do this by giving the child an appropriate outlet for his energy. This both uses up energy and engages Robert in a behavior (hitting the punching bag) that is incompatible with hitting other people.

Other parents have redirected their children's energy into less expensive but equally effective outlets like hitting a plastic pop-up Bozo toy, hitting a hard pillow, or doing jumping jacks, push-ups, or sit-ups. One mother suggested a kitchen outlet for the child's aggression:

> When my son Arthur would start to get angry and frustrated with his sister, he had a certain look and he started to move around a lot. I told him he couldn't hit his little sister, but he could hit bread dough. The harder he'd pound the dough, the better the bread would turn out. From helping me with bread, he has learned to measure ingredients and read recipes. By the age of 8, he could cook a meal from simple cookbooks.

This mother not only solved the problem of aggression but helped channel the energy into a useful skill. As in Robert's story above, these parents didn't wait until Arthur had actually hit someone. They became expert at recognizing the first steps (looking a certain way and starting to move around a lot) in the chain of behaviors that led to hitting. They found that it was easier to redirect Arthur before he got himself in trouble. They interrupted the chain of behavior as soon as they saw it beginning.

Spitting

Sometimes autistic children do not seem to have any sense of what the other person feels or experiences from their behavior. A number of parents wrote that this was apparently true for their children, who would spit at other children and adults, often spitting directly into the other person's face. Martin's story is typical:

> Something had to be done to get Martin to stop spitting in people's faces or he would not be allowed into the workshop. We worked together with his teacher, but everything we tried failed until we agreed that each time he spit we would squirt him in the face with water. The teacher did the same thing at school. Once he found out how it felt himself, he stopped.

In polite society, spitting is one of the most insulting of all gestures, but autistic children often lack the social judgment necessary to understand the seriousness of this insult. These parents have chosen to have the child understand how it feels even if he does not understand the significance of the spitting. Spitting is an aggressive behavior, although not life threatening, that often gets autistic children removed from classrooms, workshops, or group homes. These parents applied punishment quickly and consistently each time Martin spit at home or at school. Other parents said that water was not effective, and the spitting stopped only when they used vinegar or lemon juice, which they squirted directly into their son's mouth each time he spit. (The small plastic lemons that some lemon juice comes in are ideal for this purpose because they are small and can be tucked in a pocket for easy availability.)

DESTRUCTION OF PROPERTY

Another of the most stressful problems identified by parents and other family members is destruction of property by the autistic child. This ranges from breaking more obvious things such as knick knacks or other decorative items around the house, or tearing books, to disassembling major appliances, or destroying clothing or drapery, sometimes thread by thread. Parents often note that they don't think the child does this deliberately or maliciously. Often the child seems to be attracted by a dangling thread, by a flapping drape, or by shiny objects. Even if not deliberate, however, such behaviors can wreak havoc in a home.

Effective solutions parents reported include some that prevented the tearing or breaking from starting, some that redirected the child's energy and attention elsewhere, and some that changed what happened or what payoff the child received for his or her destructive behavior.

Preventing Destruction of Small Household Items

A number of parents talked of childproofing their homes by putting breakables out of sight or sometimes just out of reach.

> My 5-year-old son, Gordon, alternately roared through the house like a tornado, knocking over everything in his path, or else he continuously flipped or flicked objects from coffee tables or end tables. He never seemed to deliberately break things, but he sure was effective at it. At first we tried to put everything breakable away, but then the house had the stripped-down look of an institution. Instead, my husband decided he had a way that we could enjoy our photos and favorite things without putting them in the path of destruction. He built a narrow shelf with a low railing all around the room just above the door frames. That way we got to enjoy our favorite things, but we also kept them out of harm's way. As Gordon has gotten older (and has lost a little of his zip), we've been able to take more and more things down from our "decorator shelf" and teach him not to touch them on tables. We started doing that with some of the least fragile and least breakable things first. We've gotten so many compliments on our decorator shelf that we'll probably always want to leave some attractive things up there.

These parents found an innovative solution to their child's rampaging that solved the problem without giving their house a stripped-down "institutional" look. They provided an uncluttered, nonbreakable environment for Gordon while keeping their treasures in view. By gradually reintroducing objects, they also avoided overstimulating the child with a roomful of novel items.

Other types of preventive maintenance included buying childproof plastic cupboard locks, found in any hardware store (door pulls can't open doors until a plastic release is flipped), putting sliding bolt locks high up on doors, or putting valuable, breakable things in a locked "adult parlor." (See also the discussion on locks in Chapter 7.)

Some things are not so easily secured. Several parents engineered specially designed combination locks for dryers both to keep the child out of them and to keep the open dryer from being disassembled bolt by bolt. Another father described the childproof lock he designed for a furnace door. Although the specific lock used in each case was unique to that piece of equipment, the more general solution these parents used was preventing the damage from occurring, rather than punishing the misbehavior after injury or expensive damage had occurred.

Preventing Destruction of Books

Because many parents felt strongly that they wanted their children to use books, they decided that putting them out of the way was not a good alternative.

> Our 4-year-old son, Ethan, loves books, but began by shredding them. Each morning when we awoke, there would be a pile of shredded paper where his books had been. Not wanting to remove the books, since I wanted him to like them, I replaced them with laminated books available in any children's bookstore. The problem was solved—the pages were too thick for him to tear! After he got used to these books and came to like them, I was able to reintroduce paperbacks and other regular books without the problem recurring.

By making destruction of the books difficult, Ethan's parents eliminated the sounds and the feel of tearing that Ethan apparently enjoyed. Once he learned to enjoy laminated books properly, regular books were gradually reintroduced.

Another mother coupled a similar solution with speech and language lessons:

> My son Malcolm wouldn't look at books. Instead, he would tear them if I let him. To solve the problem, we made him a special book with pages made of artist's boards, which can't be torn. I painted his favorite things on the pages: leaves, apple, orange, banana, his three-wheeler, his hammock, ice cream, cookies. We encourage him to use the book to identify and name what he wants. He likes to turn the pages and sometimes uses speech on his own to identify the objects. Although he is still somewhat clumsy with regular books (turning pages in clumps at a time), he can now sit with us sometimes and look at a regular book without tearing it up. Somehow, making a book that worked for him— one he could turn pages in and understand—has helped him to understand why we think books are to be handled carefully.

This mother made the book meaningful to Malcolm on his terms. Previous books had been meaningless to him. In this case, Malcolm's mother gauged his appropriate developmental level and then figured out a way to help her son understand at that level what a book was and how to use it. This also helped to develop a communication system for him, and the book became a source of reinforcers for Malcolm as he was able to use it to get what he wanted—ice cream, his three-wheeler, and so on. The book then became as valuable to Malcolm as other books were to his mother. Adults read books and value them because they are a source of knowledge, excitement, and adventure. Since Malcolm couldn't read, he couldn't value books for these reasons. His mother found a way to make books meaningful and rewarding to her son by adjusting the book to his developmental level.

A further extension of this idea of owning his own books was suggested by Jack's mother, as reported in Chapter 4 (p. 72).

Preventing Destruction of Furniture

A number of parents reported that their child had destroyed major pieces of furniture by jumping on them. Many different parents have found out on their own (or learned from other parents) about solutions like the one reported by a parent in Chapter 4 (p. 76). Both 11-year-old Eugene and 17-year-old Jim caused damage by excessive jumping on the sofa. Both boys learned to release their energy instead on a trampoline. Eugene's mother not only stopped the destruction, but gave her son some status in the neighborhood as well. Finding an activity at which the autistic child can be successful is often a first step toward encouraging interaction with other children. Jim's father noted the expense involved:

> I finally thought of getting a small jogging trampoline ($22-$60, depending on store and size), which Jim loves. Although a trampoline only lasts about 1 year with Jim, it saves the furniture. It also keeps Jim in shape and provides an outlet for his energy and a free-time activity. Jim also knows that when he has a lot of energy to burn off, he can go to the trampoline. This has been a help, especially in the winter when it is difficult to get out as much.

Instead of consigning the trampoline to distant places, other parents have put the "bouncer" near whatever piece of furniture (e.g., bed, sofa) the child formerly jumped on, so that any move in that direction could be immediately redirected onto the bouncer.

One family had an "olympic class" jumper, so they decided to develop the jumping into a polished leisure activity.

> My 4-year-old daughter, Mae, discovered it was great fun to climb the fence and jump up and down on the roof of my husband's car. I tried every approach I could think of to stop her but to no avail. Given 60 seconds unattended, she would scale the fence and be doing the Chevy Stomp again. Finally, I telephoned every gymnasium in town until I found a gymnast who would give my daughter a private lesson on the trampoline once a week. She immediately became skilled at it, stopped jumping on the car, and to my surprise and delight, said her first sentence.

The importance of adequate physical activity was stressed by many parents. Parents wrote of the calming effects of having aggressive children jog or do jumping jacks or other exercises that did not require special equipment (see also Chapter 4, Play and Leisure, for physical exercise ideas).

Preventing Destruction of Clothing

One recurring concern of parents of autistic children is that their children destroy clothes by chewing or tearing them.

> Andrew continually bit the front of his shirt so that all his clothes had holes. I couldn't keep up with the mending or the cost of replacing them. Finally, I put tabasco sauce on the front of his shirt in the spot where he usually chewed it. It burned his mouth when he chewed, and as a result, he stopped the chewing.

Instead of the reinforcing sensation of chewing, the child's mouth burned when he chewed his shirt. Another resourceful parent used liquid soap instead of tabasco sauce. It was distasteful to the child but didn't stain the shirt. Another mother used a hot-tasting, colorless liquid designed to stop thumb sucking to get her daughter to stop chewing the thumbs out of all her mittens.

A final clothing protection idea was suggested by a mother whose son tore his clothing:

My son Jeff was a clothing shredder. No matter what he had on, he eventually figured out a way to tear it into strips. This was especially a problem with shirts and shorts. I finally had him wear clothes made of denim that were too strong for him to tear. He had kind of a cowboy look for a while, but it prevented him from ruining his clothes and looking like something the ragman dropped off.

This mother, like the mothers who used posterboard for books, eliminated the destructive behavior by making the material itself childproof. By changing the environment in this way, they eliminated the behavior by making it impossible to occur. Once they broke the tearing habit, they were able to reintroduce other materials.

Parents, then, used a variety of creative ideas to eliminate self-injury, aggression against others, and destruction of property. Some of these interventions are similar to those suggested in the research literature. Professionals have often stressed the importance of reducing the payoff for self-injurious behavior—for example, by withdrawing positive attention or other positive influences for the behavior. Many interventions designed by parents to protect their children also served to eliminate the positive payoff for the child's behavior. In the limited sample of parent solutions presented here, most parents concentrated on changing the environment rather than the child. The solutions they proposed were often aimed at maintaining a semblance of a normal home and at not interfering with normal family life. Many of the procedures in the research literature are time consuming and physically demanding. While parents have the luxury of interrupting a relatively new behavior, their solutions, if applied frequently and consistently, hold promise of preventing more serious and more dangerous habits from developing.

REFERENCES

Berkson, G., & Mason, W. A. (1964). Stereotyped movements of mental defectives, IV: The effects of toys and the character of the acts. *American Journal of Mental Deficiencies, 68,* 511–524.

Cataldo, M. F., & Harris, J. (1982). The biological basis for self-injury in the mentally retarded. *Analysis and Intervention in Developmental Disabilities, 2,* 21–39.

Favell, J. E., McGimsey, J. F., & Jones, M. L. (1978). The use of physical restraining in the treatment of self-injury and as positive reinforcement. *Journal of Applied Behavior Analysis, 11,* 225–241.

Favell, J. E., McGimsey, J. F., & Schnell, R. M. (1982). Treatment of self-injury by providing alternate sensory activities. *Analysis and Intervention in Developmental Disabilities, 2,* 83–104.

MacLean, W. E., & Baumeister, A. A. (1982). Effects of vestibular stimulation on motor development and stereotyped behavior of developmentally delayed children. *Journal of Abnormal Child Psychology, 10,* 229–245.

Mulick, J. A., & Durand, J. R. (1989). Antisocial behavior, aggression, and delinquency. In *Treatment of psychiatric disorders* (Vol. 1, pp. 20–26). Washington, DC: American Psychiatric Disorders.

Saposnek, D. T., & Watson, L. S. (1974). The elimination of the self-destructive behavior of a psychotic child: A case study. *Behavior Therapy, 5,* 79–89.

Schroeder, S. R., Rohajn, J., & Mulick, J. (1978). Ecobehavioral organization of developmental day care for the chronically self-injurious. *Journal of Pediatric Psychology, 3,* 81–88.

Schroeder, S. R., Schroeder, C. S., Rojahn, J., & Mulick, J. (1981). Self-injurious behavior: An analysis of behavior management techniques. In J. L. Matson & J. R. McCarthey (Eds.), *Handbook of behavior modification with the mentally retarded* (pp. 61–115). New York: Plenum Press.

Wells, M., & Smith, D. W. (1983). Reduction of self-injurious behavior of mentally retarded persons using sensory integrative techniques. *American Journal of Mental Deficiency, 87,* 664–666.

6

Toileting and Hygiene

Problem Behaviors

Underlying Deficits

M uch of the stress that parents of autistic and developmentally handicapped children experience comes from their children's prolonged dependence on them. Often their children are unable to eat, toilet, dress, and wash independently. This places extreme demands on the parents' time and energy, and can be a source of embarrassment for them. The lack of basic toileting and hygiene skills can also lead to health problems for the children.

To acquire toileting and hygiene skills, children need to learn a number of complex discriminations and motor sequences. This is difficult for children with autism because of their poor motor planning and failure to pick up on social cues. In addition, such children may be very sensitive to the smells, tastes, or textures involved in toileting and hygiene. Most professionals approach these problems by breaking the tasks into small parts and systematically teaching the necessary skills by using operant conditioning techniques (Ando, 1977; Azrin & Foxx, 1971) or special education. These programs are often carried out in institutions where conditions can be controlled and regular schedules are easily maintained. Many of these studies have been conducted with mentally retarded subjects with whom success was heavily dependent on the effect of social praise and criticism. The use of social praise and criticism is often less effective for people with autism. Also, these techniques are not always relevant to their particular sensitivities and behavioral quirks. In the following sections, parents present solutions to problems they encountered when teaching their children self-help skills.

TOILETING

That their child can't go to the toilet independently places an extra strain on the families of autistic children. Inability to remain clean and dry is not accepted in the community, and is embarrassing for the family and unhealthy for the child. Cleaning up accidents and monitoring toileting procedures can take up much time and energy. When toileting problems persist beyond early childhood, they can impair parents' morale and lifestyle.

There are many reasons why children with autism may fail to develop independent toileting skills at an early age. Failure to develop these skills may result from delays in physical and mental development (Bettison, 1978). Independent toileting involves controlling bodily functions, making decisions about where it is appropriate to relieve oneself, and having the self-help skills to undress and dress oneself. These all require certain levels of physiological maturation as well as mental development. Children with pervasive developmental disorder often have behaviors that can create obstacles to toilet training. The following parents' coping strategies for solving such problems range from the commonsense to the imaginative. Each solution is forged from the interaction of their unique child with his or her particular home environment.

Controlling Bodily Functions

The first major step in a toilet-training program is often to help the child recognize his or her own body processes. Bettison (1978) pointed out that many handicapped children who are not toilet trained may not have reached the level of neuromuscular maturation needed to perceive that their bladder is full. Thus, they may urinate in their clothing without awareness. Clearly, this is the case for some young autistic children. One mother reports:

> When Jim was 3, I began to toilet train him. I wasn't succeeding, because
> . he didn't seem to realize when he would urinate—he didn't recognize the
> sensation. I noticed that standing at the window and watching the leaves
> on the tree outside stimulated him to urinate. So, I rolled up the rug and
> put the potty seat by the front window. Every time he started to urinate,
> I put him on the potty (I took his training pants off so that he could see

what was happening). After the first week, I put his training pants back on, and in 2 weeks he was completely trained!

This mother taught her son to make the connection between the physical act of urinating and the proper place to do it. To speed up this process, she took advantage of his natural interest in the leaves and his tendency to urinate while watching the leaves. She provided many opportunities for practice by moving his potty seat to the front window, the place where he was most likely to urinate.

To help mentally retarded children become more attuned to their body processes, researchers have devised signal-alarm systems. These devices are installed in the child's pants and give off a signal when touched by urine. Once the child has learned to go to the toilet in response to the alarm signal, the trainers gradually fade out the alarm. However, this is not enough for some children. The following is an example of a child who does not know what to do after being brought to the toilet.

> Brian, age 3½, wasn't toilet trained or able to speak. On the advice of a professional, I took off his diaper and sat him backward on the toilet. I kept a treat in my pocket to reward him if he went in the toilet. I had no success with this until I involved my husband. When he came home and had to go to the bathroom, I quickly took Brian into the bathroom so that he could watch my husband. When my husband urinated in the toilet, I gave him a treat and said good boy and hugged him. Brian got the idea right away and followed my husband's example. From that day on, Brian has been toilet trained.

The professional apparently thought that Brian was failing to urinate because he felt insecure, and that sitting him backward on the toilet would help him to feel more secure. The mother concluded that Brian did not understand verbal directions of what to do, and therefore needed his father's modeling. Once he understood what to do, he began to urinate in the toilet.

Many toilet-training programs designed by professionals involve the elements mentioned above: bringing the child to the toilet at regular intervals, using a positive reinforcer for any appropriate urination, and giving verbal praise. The purpose behind these procedures is to help the child make the connection between the act of urinating and the appropriate place to do it. Punishment is avoided whenever possible. However, some success has also been reported by having the child clean himself or herself and the soiled items after having an accident. This commonsense solution has been used by many parents who have found that their children become more careful when they learn that if they make a mess, they have to clean it up.

> My autistic son, Victor, is 10 years old and tends to wet the bed every once in a while. When this happens, I tell him to take everything off the bed, and then I wash it. When he returns home from school, I tell him to make the bed and show him how. It seems to work to control the wetting.

Here the mother has Victor help clean up his mess. However, she adjusts it to his developmental level by not having him do the washing. Instead, she asks him to remove the soiled sheets. The mother also uses the bed wetting as an opportunity to practice self-help skills, by teaching him how to make his bed.

Going in the Right Place

Once children have begun to recognize their body signals, they need to learn the appropriate place to urinate. Most successful toilet-training programs involve a component of teaching a child to go to the toilet in response to having a full bladder. These training programs approach teaching this skill in different ways. Some use a bell or buzzer that goes off as soon as a child begins to wet his or her pants. The trainer then immediately brings the child to the toilet. Others have recommended that the child sit on the toilet at regularly scheduled intervals. The child is then rewarded for urinating appropriately. Some of these methods may be taxing for parents to carry out at home. Most parents help the children by making a direct connection between voiding and going to the toilet.

> As a small child, Gena would pull her pants down and go to the bathroom on the floor or on the carpet. The parents responded by immediately bringing her to the toilet. This was to help her make the connection between the act of urinating and the toilet. Later, they made her clean her mess up. The combination of bringing her to the toilet and having her clean her mess up eventually succeeded in getting her toilet trained.

Some children don't seem to realize that there is an appropriate place for them to relieve themselves.

> When Reggie was 5, he wasn't toilet trained. I noticed that when he had diapers or training pants on, he'd wet them, but he never urinated when he had nothing on—as if he were scared to. So one day I took the diapers off. When he started "twirling around in desperation" I forced him to sit on the toilet. Screaming all the while, he finally urinated and noticed that he didn't get wet. From that point on, he was toilet trained.

Initially, it seemed that Reggie had two problems: first, that he didn't know the proper place to go to the toilet, and second, that his sensory integration was not developed enough to recognize that he urinated when he had diapers on to absorb the urine. His mother's solution was to remove the diaper, thereby forcing him to be aware of urinating. This scared the boy until he realized that the toilet was a place where he could urinate and not get wet. Thus, by bringing him to the toilet, Reggie's mother succeeded in toilet training him and increasing his sensory awareness.

Some males manage to get themselves to the toilet but urinate on the floor as well as in the toilet. One professional helped focus urination by using a target in the toilet. He placed a toy boat or luminescent ball in the toilet and instructed boys to urinate. He found that boys tended to aim at the target, and thus, urinate completely in the toilet. Parents have come up with similar solutions.

> Juan, age 4, had poor aim while urinating. We put a fishing line floater in the tank and told him to aim at that. We noticed that he enjoyed aiming at the float and that his aim improved.

These parents concluded their son was missing the toilet because he was not sufficiently attentive. The fishing line floater attracted his attention and helped to focus him while urinating. This was all that Juan needed to improve his aim.

Related Self-Help Skills

Some children are held back from independent toileting because they lack the necessary self-help skills. Most comprehensive toilet-training programs recognize this and include dressing and undressing

skills. Successful toileting programs usually break the act of toileting
into steps: walk to the toilet, remove clothing, sit on the toilet, complete
elimination, replace clothing, and return to a favored activity. This
program emphasizes teaching one step at a time. The child is not
considered toilet trained until all the steps are mastered in their proper
order. Initially, it may be necessary to prompt the child with each step
and then gradually fade out the prompts as they are no longer needed.
Such teaching programs work for most children. However, some
children continue to have problems. A parent offers this quick and easy
solution:

> Jason is potty trained but cannot undo belts, zippers, and buttons. To
> allow him go to the bathroom by himself, I bought him jogging pants
> (sweatpants) with an elastic waist. Since he only has to pull these up and
> down, he is able to dress himself independently.

Jason's lack of dressing skills prevented him from being completely independent at toileting, even though he was toilet trained. His
mother circumvented the problem by finding a solution that provided
him with independence—jogging pants. In the long run, he will be
more independent if he can unfasten belts and buttons. In the meantime,
jogging pants buy a bit more time needed for learning buckles and
buttons. Velcro fasteners have also been used.

Behavioral Obstacles to Toilet Training

In the process of training autistic children, parents often encounter
unusual obstacles. Children may be fascinated by certain aspects of
objects and become so engrossed in these details that they forget what
they were supposed to do. In other instances, a child may be bothered
by the texture or smell of an object and refuse to comply with a request.
With a young child, this resistance may take the form of an extreme
fear or avoidance of a particular object. The professional literature
describes cases of "toilet phobia," in which children showed extreme
fear of going to the toilet. A number of approaches have been used to
overcome this, such as reinforcing these children for going near the
toilet and systematically presenting them with certain aspects of the
toilet. For example, sitting on the toilet to look at a favorite book
gradually helps him or her grow accustomed to the sound of flushing.

As parents become accustomed to observing their child, they find increasing numbers of creative solutions to such problems. In our experience, parents often independently develop coping skills that are similar to behavior techniques published in technical professional journals.

> When Paul was 4, he wouldn't sit on the toilet seat. We tried adjusting the height of the toilet, but he still refused to sit on it. Finally, we bought a soft commode seat, and from that point on, Paul would sit down without balking.

Paul apparently was affected by the texture of the toilet seat. His parents overcame that obstacle through a process of trial and error and careful observation of their son's behavior. Instead of coaxing Paul to comply, they searched for the reason for his discomfort and eventually solved the problem.

> Our young son Andy, age 4, had just been potty trained. In the process of being trained, he began to play in the toilet water. Since I couldn't get him to stop unless I stayed with him, I put the potty chair right into the toilet. This helped him to use the toilet and prevented him from being able to play in the water.

This parent decided that rather than punishing Andy for playing in the toilet water, she would change the environment to prevent him from playing in the water. She felt that it was most important for Andy to be able to go to the toilet independently, so she created a situation that allowed him to do that.

> With urine training completed at age 4½, we could no longer lock Marc from the bathroom. He became fascinated with flushing the toilet and playing with things on the shelves and in the medicine cabinet. Marc learned he could stand on the back of the commode to reach forbidden objects. I then decided to take the removable back off to prevent him from climbing up. This allows him to go to the toilet without us having to watch him.

As in the previous anecdote, Marc became toilet trained but still could not be trusted to go to the bathroom independently. His mother solved that problem by removing his means of reaching forbidden objects.

A related problem developed in a group home for adolescents and adults. Roger stayed in the bathroom for long periods of time, preventing others from using it. The group home manager found this solution to the problem.

> Roger, who is 20, lives in a group home and monopolizes the bathroom in the mornings. So now the staff sets a timer when he goes into the bathroom. Roger loves to eat a big breakfast, particularly pancakes and sausage. If he gets out of the bathroom before the timer goes off, he gets to choose what he wants for breakfast. If he gets out after the timer goes off, he must eat what everyone else does.

Generally, Roger was successful and could choose his breakfast menu. The staff capitalized on his strong motivation for food to solve a problem behavior. Since Roger had difficulty understanding how his monopolizing the bathroom was affecting other people, the staff used the timer as a concrete way to let him know when he had taken too long in the bathroom.

Coping with Embarrassment

Having a child who is not toilet trained at an appropriate age can be very embarrassing for parents and siblings. Most autistic children lack the social awareness to be embarrassed themselves. However, some parents remain at home in order to avoid the anxiety of their child wetting his or her pants in public. Parents may sense disapproval from relatives and friends, and thus refrain from joining in family gatherings or even having people come over to their homes. Some parents have come up with simple solutions to these problems, and thus have been able to take their children out in public places.

> Our 8-year-old son Pablo's toilet training was a little shaky for many years. We found that dressing him in black or navy blue pants, especially when going on outings, was best. If he did have an accident, it was much less noticeable.

These parents coped well with the embarrassment of Pablo's wet pants by eliminating the public effects of the problem. With the dark pants, their son could have an accident, and they weren't embarrassed by it. This enabled them to go out in public as they pleased, reducing their frustration.

> In toilet training Vickie, we had no success in following the "traditional" idea of having her wear training pants all day. We became quite tired of cleaning up carpets, upholstered furniture, and so on. We also began to be bothered by the fact that Vickie was constantly wet in public. By the time she was 5, we were ready to abandon the toilet-training program, when it was suggested that we switch to Pampers instead of training pants. Cleanup is no longer a problem, embarrassment in public disappeared, and training is succeeding nicely.

These parents were frustrated and embarrassed with Vickie's lack of independent toileting skills. This frustration was so great that they were ready to give up the toilet-training program. Instead, they decided to switch from training pants to Pampers. This relieved their frustration by eliminating the most negative effects of their daughter's accidents: creating messes in the home and embarrassing her parents in public. Once these frustrations were lessened, the parents were able to continue with Vickie's toilet-training program in a more relaxed and successful manner.

Smearing

Another problem related to toilet training is the smearing or eating of feces. This problem can occur with both successfully trained and untrained children. Smearing is unattractive and difficult to deal with. Parents and caregivers often feel ashamed or disgusted at their child's behavior. Often the adults' reactions to smearing are punitive and ineffective. Some parents have found more effective solutions.

> When Anita was 4, she would remove her clothes and smear feces. Nothing that we tried was successful at eliminating the problem. Finally, we bought long-sleeved jumpsuit coveralls and put them on her backward with the zipper in the back. This eliminated the problem. Eventually, we were able to dress her in normal clothing.

Instead of looking for a psychological or emotional cause for their daughter's smearing, these parents settled on a practical deterrent. They put the coveralls on backward, so that their daughter was unable to get at her feces when she had an accident in her pants. This prevented her from smearing. Over time, Anita was toilet trained, the problem disappeared, and Anita was able to wear normal clothing.

As a young child, Ann would smear feces when she went to the bathroom. We gave her a limited amount of time in the bathroom, had someone accompany her each time she went, and took her out of the bathroom as soon as she was finished. This helped the behavior to disappear.

These parents decided to closely monitor their daughter's behavior instead of punishing or restricting her. By accompanying her into the bathroom, they could structure Ann's actions and prevent the smearing from occurring.

Professionals have tried a variety of approaches to smearing and eating feces. Most traditional approaches involved using restraints. Some have used an overcorrection procedure. With one child, this included having her brush her teeth, wash her hands, and clean the floor for 10-minute periods each time she was found to have eaten feces. This reduced her undesirable behavior dramatically, and at the same time improved her toothbrushing skills. A more positive approach was used by another professional. A 7-year-old patient who smeared feces seemed to enjoy the attention he received from staff when they punished him for this behavior. They charted his behavior and found that his smearing generally occurred in the 2-hour period before his shower. The problem was solved by changing his shower schedule so that he took showers at an earlier time and by allowing him to play longer in the shower.

Sometimes an underlying problem for smearing feces can be identified. For example, a physical examination can reveal that the child is constipated or has difficulty passing his or her stool. Stool softeners and other treatments for constipation may solve this problem.

Chuck smeared feces on the walls until he was 7. Since he suffered from chronic constipation, our doctor prescribed enemas every 3 days. However, he didn't think there was any other physical problem related to the smearing. We went to another doctor to get a second opinion. He examined Chuck and prescribed some medication. Chuck's constipation went away, and with it the smearing disappeared.

It seems that the smearing was related to Chuck's constipation. The discomfort that he felt from the constipation caused him to stick his hand in his rectal area, which eventually led to smearing. The enemas were painful for the child and troublesome for the parents to give; medication is a much more pleasant cure for constipation. Once Chuck's constipation was relieved, the cause of the smearing was eliminated and the smearing disappeared.

With many young children, smearing feces is associated with boredom and too much unstructured time alone. This is readily stopped by reducing the cause.

HYGIENE

A developmentally handicapped child's lack of independent hygiene skills can be very stressful to his or her parents. Unlike vocational or academic tasks, hygiene tasks *must* be carried out several times each day. Improper toothbrushing or washing can become a health hazard and jeopardize a child's participation in community activities. Unclean or unkempt children are often rejected socially from participating in community groups. The strong social value attributed to these self-care skills contributes to feelings of frustration and anger of parents whose children resist personal hygiene or are unable to clean themselves.

There are some professional programs designed to teach hygiene skills by breaking them into a series of small steps. Children are taught these steps one at a time until they master the entire sequence (Wehman, 1979). Rewards are often used to motivate children to learn skills that are not intrinsically rewarding. Structured teaching methods are often effective. However, the children may have peculiar characteristics that interfere with the use of such programs, unless individual adaptations are found. For example, abnormal functioning of their sensory modalities causes many autistic children to have unusual reactions to temperature, taste, or texture. Such individualization is reflected in the parents' anecdotes where successful solutions depend on understanding the underlying problems.

Bathing

Many autistic children do not like to bathe themselves. They do not understand or care about the health or social consequences of being dirty. Further, the skills involved in independent bathing are difficult for these children to learn. They have to acquire the abilities to regulate water temperature, scrub themselves until they are clean, and then rinse and dry themselves. Most professionals have used a mixture of teaching techniques, including breaking each part of bathing into even smaller tasks, using pictures of body parts, and demonstrating the separate skills. Since concepts such as hot and cold are difficult to understand, color-coded faucets have been used to help children practice touching water of various temperatures before they enter the bathtub.

Many autistic children can learn to regulate the water but resist or are incapable of washing themselves. This may be caused, among other things, by sensitivity to being scrubbed, the texture of the soap, fear of water spray, or difficulty in coordinating the actions. One mother reported:

> I was having a difficult time getting my 6-year-old daughter, Cortney, to wash herself. She enjoys water, but would not use the washcloth to clean herself. At the suggestion of a therapist, I made Cortney a mitten out of a washcloth to use in the tub. Since she liked pictures, I also cut out pictures of various body parts and laminated them. I now point to the picture of the body part I want her to wash and sign "wash" and she does it.

This parent combined two ideas to get her daughter to wash herself. The mitt made it physically easier for Cortney to wash herself. The pictures helped structure the bathing process, enabling the mother to give clear directions to wash one body part at a time. Rinsing can also be aided by using a shower extension. This flexible hand-held hose allows the child to control the water and avoid getting sprayed in the face.

A simple solution to the problem of tactile sensitivity was suggested by another parent.

> Jack does not like to wash himself. He will not use a washcloth or lather up with a bar of soap. This problem was solved when we switched to liquid soap in a dispenser. I squirted a small amount in each hand and rubbed his hands together. Then I taught him to rub it on his body to get the soap off his hands and to wash himself. I directed his hands by holding his arms. When he had rubbed the soap all over his body, I let him rinse it off. This allowed him to clean himself.

Jack was apparently bothered by the tactile sensation of holding something in his hands. His mother observed this problem when he used either a washcloth or bar soap. In using the liquid soap, she capitalized on Jack's tactile sensitivity by showing him that he could get the soap off of his hands by rubbing it all over his body. Thus, she used his tactile sensitivity to teach Jack how to wash himself by using liquid soap that he had to rub off his hands rather than bar soap that he could drop at will.

It is difficult to explain to autistic children what it means to be clean. Children may go through the motions of scrubbing themselves without having any sense of purpose. One parent found a wonderful nonverbal solution to this problem.

Maria, age 7, would not attempt to wash herself in the tub. Her mother used a colorful liquid soap in a bottle with a roll-on top (from Avon) to "color" Maria's arms, legs, chest, and so on. Maria would wash the soap off with a wash rag. Thus, Maria completed the task of washing her body by herself.

Maria did not understand the concept of being clean. The colored soap helped focus her attention on different parts of her body and identified where she should scrub herself. This made the process of washing herself interesting and understandable to her, enabling her to do it by herself.

A pet peeve of many children is having their hair washed. Parents often find it difficult to get their children comfortable enough to allow them to shampoo their hair easily. One professional (Robinault, 1973) suggests placing the child in a bath seat made by cutting out part of a rubber laundry basket. The basket is placed in the bathtub and provides a seat for the child to sit in. This provides stability for the child and makes hair washing safer. A parent suggested a similar solution.

David, age 5, hated to have his hair washed. He never felt secure when tilted backward. Add to this an abnormal sensitivity to anyone touching his neck, and hair washing became an acrobatic feat. We solved the problem by stripping an old infant carrier seat of its fabric and placing it in the bathtub. David was totally supported in the lowest position, and his head was in the right position to keep water and soap from his eyes. Best of all, no one had to touch his neck in the process.

These parents decided that David balked at having his hair washed for two reasons: sensitivity to having his neck touched and fear when his head was tilted backward in the tub. When placed in the child carrier seat, David felt safe. Since this position also allowed his parents to wash his hair without having to touch his neck, David was able to relax enough for his parents to wash his hair.

Perhaps the most basic bathing obstacle is coping with children who are afraid to enter the bathtub.

> My son Carver was afraid of the bathtub. When he was 4, he would scream and howl every time we tried to get him in the tub. We had him watch our neighbor's little boy take a bath. Soon, Carver showed an interest in the tub and would get in with the other little boy. Finally, we were able to get him in the tub by himself.

This is a good example of how modeling can be used as an effective technique to teach a desired behavior. Watching the other little boy helped this child become less afraid of the tub, and in effect, showed him what to do. It also helped promote social interaction by getting the two boys in the tub together.

Other children were able to get used to immersing their body in water gradually.

> Abel, age 5, was afraid to get in the bath. We put his favorite toy in a bucket of water and asked him to get it out. This let him practice touching the water. Gradually, we began to fill the tub to low levels and have Abel pull out his toys. Soon he was able to get in the tub with his toys, which allowed us to give him a bath.

Abel was afraid of the water. By placing his favorite toy in the bucket of water, he was motivated enough to come into contact with an unpleasant stimulus (the water). His parents gradually got him used to touching the water in the bathtub. Over time, the amount of water was increased until it was enough for Abel to take a bath in. This gradual process enabled the boy to overcome his fear slowly and helped his parents to give him a bath.

Toothbrushing

Many children, with or without handicaps, do not like to brush their teeth at first. Autistic children often are afraid of brushing their teeth, and seem to be particularly sensitive to having the brush rub their gums. Since children with developmental handicaps cannot understand why they need to brush their teeth, it is important to recognize their fears and find ways to reduce them. One good idea is to use a soft toothbrush. Another helpful idea is to have the child watch adults brushing their teeth and then look in the mirror while brushing his or her own teeth.

As with bathing, toothbrushing programs tend to break down the procedure into small steps (Horner & Keilitz, 1975). At first, a great deal of help is required, including physical assistance. Over time, this assistance is slowly reduced until the child can complete all the steps independently. However, many of these steps are difficult for some children because of their poor fine-motor coordination. For children who have difficulty holding onto a toothbrush, elastic strips can be used to help strap the brush to their hands. Other children may grip the toothbrush, but be unable to hold it solidly as they brush. Under this condition, the handle may be extended by attaching bicycle grips, foil, or styrofoam to it (Saunders, 1976; Schopler, Reichler, & Lansing, 1980). Yet, some children continue to resist the best of established, professional toothbrushing aides. One parent told this anecdote:

> Brushing teeth used to be dreaded in our home. It was a fight from start to finish and our autistic son, Lon, age 6, would take a while to wind down after the "ordeal." In January I found fruit-flavored fluoride toothpaste. Not only does Lon enjoy it but he now reminds us to "brush teeth." If you'd like to try it, the address of the makers of the toothpaste is J. R. Research Inc., Salt Lake City, UT 84107.

For a long time, these parents found toothbrushing to be a battle, and they had to force Lon to brush his teeth. Finally, they decided that he did not like the taste of the toothpaste. They solved this problem by switching to the fruit-flavored toothpaste, and toothbrushing became a rewarding experience for him.

Other children require other unique forms of extra motivation to brush their teeth willingly.

> Sarah, who was 6, didn't like to put her toothbrush in her mouth. We turned toothbrushing into a game—Mom would sing a song while Sarah brushed. When Mom got to certain lines in the song, it provided a cue for Sarah to move her brush to a different part of her mouth.

Ethan, an adolescent, hated toothbrushing. His favorite game was
having someone say "3-2-1- . . . blastoff." His teachers made a game out
of toothbrushing by counting down (10, 9, 8, . . .) while he brushed. This
got him excited and prompted him to brush his teeth.

These two innovative solutions are similar. In each case, the parent
or teacher responded to an unpleasurable event by combining it with
something that was pleasurable for the child. This helped make
toothbrushing more fun, turning what had been a dreaded activity into
an enjoyable one.

Another mother used her son's special interests to help improve
his dental care.

I've had many problems getting dental work done on my autistic
son. Dan, who is 9, brushes carelessly or simply chews on the brush
a minute or two. He has a fascination with strings, so I was able to get
him into flossing. I purchased a Water Pik, and it is the treat of the
day for him to use this with a fluoride mouthwash that he normally
wouldn't use.

This mother managed to capitalize on some of her son's special
interests in order to improve Dan's dental care. Dan obviously was
disinterested in toothbrushing and did a poor job. Instead of fighting
with him, she used her imagination and his interest in strings to teach
him how to use dental floss. The Water Pik allowed Dan to rinse his
gums without having to hold mouthwash in his mouth as one would
normally have to do. It was also fun for him to squirt the mouthwash
through the hose and to hear the motor of the Water Pik run.

Getting a child to the dentist can be difficult because many autistic
children are afraid of going to the dentist.

Our 7-year-old son, Jerry, is terrified of going to the dentist. He once had
a cavity filled, which was an unpleasant experience for him. We have
arranged with a dentist for Jerry to go for a few friendly visits. This
dentist will show him the different tools and equipment and let him play
with them. Not until the third or fourth visit does the dentist clean Jerry's
teeth. This has made trips to the dentist quite pleasant.

This excellent idea turned a frightening activity into a pleasant
one. Exploring the tools and equipment was fun for Jerry and made him

less afraid when the dentist actually used the tools for dental care. Since most children with autism will not understand verbal explanations, allowing them to touch and play with the equipment makes the dentist's office a less confusing and terrifying place.

Grooming

Techniques similar to those used to teach bathing and toothbrushing are used to teach grooming skills. The most prevalent professional teaching techniques are demonstration and the use of task analysis. While these techniques are often effective, it has been observed that many autistic people's grooming skills are not as good as their other self-help skills. A possible explanation for this is that less emphasis is placed on teaching grooming than the more fundamental skills, such as washing and toothbrushing. Also, most developmentally handicapped people lack the social awareness to be concerned about the finer points of their appearance, such as their hair and fingernail care.

Autistic people's fears or sensitivities may stand in the way of their learning grooming skills. At times, those fears may be even strong enough to keep them from letting others assist in grooming.

> Andy does not like to get his hair cut. The shop we go to has arranged a schedule so that his father sits alongside him while they both get a haircut. This helps Andy to stay calm and allows the barber to cut his hair. This would also work using a brother or sister as the model instead of a parent.

Andy responded to the example provided by a familiar person, his father. By watching his father getting his hair cut, Andy could feel secure enough to relax and allow the barber to cut his hair.

> My son Henry, a 9-year-old, hated to have his fingernails cut. I bathe him first to soften the nails. After I cut them, I rub lotion in them, which seems to soothe him.

Having one's nails cut can be scary for an autistic child. Softening the nails made it easier for his mother to cut them, and less frightening and painful for Henry. The lotion seems to serve as a reward: Since Henry enjoys having the lotion rubbed into his fingers, it gives him something to look forward to after having his nails cut.

It is noteworthy that many of the techniques for developing these skills are also used with young children without any developmental problems. Special adaptations are usually needed for each child's individual peculiarities.

REFERENCES

Ando, H. (1977). Training autistic children to urinate in toilet through operant conditioning techniques. *Journal of Autism and Developmental Disorders, 7*, 151–163.

Azrin, N. H., & Foxx, R. (1971). A rapid method of toilet training the institutionalized retarded. *Journal of Applied Behavioral Analysis, 4*, 89–99.

Bettison, S. (1978). Toilet training the retarded: An analysis of the stages of development and procedures for designing programs. *Australian Journal of Developmental Disabilities, 5*, 95–100.

Horner, R. D., & Keilitz, I. (1975). Training mentally retarded adolescents to brush their teeth. *Journal of Applied Behavior Analysis, 8*, 301–310.

Robinault, I. P. (1973). *Functional aides for the multiply handicapped.* Hagerstown, MD: Harper & Row.

Saunders, R. H. (1976). Take a giant step to independent living: Adaptive toothbrushing. *Teaching Exceptional Children, 9*, 7.

Schopler, E., Reichler, R. J. & Lansing, M. D. (1980). *Individualized assessment and treatment for autistic and developmentally disabled children, Volume 2: Teaching strategies for parents and professionals* (2nd ed.). Austin, TX: Pro-Ed.

Wehman, P. (1979). *Curriculum design for the severely and profoundly handicapped.* New York: Human Sciences Press.

7

Eating and Sleeping

**Problem
Behaviors**

**Underlying
Deficits**

S tressful eating and sleeping patterns are not limited to autistic children. From birth to age 2½ years, all children progress through developmental stages that are clearly explained in child-rearing manuals (Brazelton, 1974; Spock & Rothenberg, 1985) and understood and expected by their parents. Unfortunately, children do not read these manuals and can find too many ways to do it in their own way. This can often be seen in how they gradually learn to feed themselves, try new foods, not eat inedibles, and imitate and accept some rules for table manners. Similarly, it is not unusual for them to dislike leaving their parents to go to sleep alone, to wake in the night and wander around, and to wake up earlier than others would like.

According to some of our guiding manuals, these behaviors are expected, understood, and felt to be tolerable because the children grow out of them. Parents know that before long they can begin to explain rules and reasons to their child. They can begin to use sensible consequences and pleasant rewards as their child begins to develop self-control and remembers his or her parents' commands. They have already seen that their child wants to please them and enjoys their affectionate praise. In addition, parents take young children to their pediatrician or family doctor frequently and again are reassured that the somewhat stressful eating and sleeping behaviors are going to get better naturally, require no special behavioral techniques, and are not a cause for worry.

Unfortunately, these so-called normal developmental sequences are more uneven or develop at a slower rate with children who have developmental handicaps. Autistic characteristics reviewed in the introduction can be involved. Children's deficits in communication skills and in understanding what their parents are telling them interferes with normal child-training techniques. Children's social deficits can block out perceptions and appreciation of praise and reduce their motivation to comply with the requests they do understand. Uneven development, with physical and motor abilities developing much faster than cognitive abilities, means that they can get out of their cribs, get out of doors, open the refrigerator, grab food, and pick up inedibles long before they have developed self-control, a memory for rules, or the ability to predict consequences. Unusual responses to taste, smell, and touch often remain fixed and intense. Finally, resistance to change combined with ritualistic behavior can make child-training efforts more difficult and unpleasant. Parents who grow tired of waiting for normal developmental changes to occur and who begin to pressure their child to "grow up" may be met with tantrums, refusals, or other forms of negative behavior.

Tense and stressful responses are often problematic when it is time for meals or sleep. Parents want their child to feel secure and relaxed at bedtime. They expect their child to feel happy and relaxed at mealtime to encourage a good appetite and enjoyment of food. Because behavioral techniques initially provoke resistance from the child and thus increase tension, many parents delay in using behavioral techniques that they may be willing to use for other activities where compliance is needed, such as dressing, toileting, or aggression. The following parent reports illustrate how they coped with their children's special challenges to eating and sleeping.

EATING

In this section, we review anecdotal material for coping with eating inedibles, picky eating, overeating, eating too fast, limited self-feeding skills, and allergic responses. One additional problem, rumination (the habit of regurgitating, chewing, and reswallowing food), was not mentioned by parents, but is referred to frequently in the literature (Schroeder, 1989). This probably occurs more often in institutional settings than at home, but it is also included.

Eating Inedibles

The following five parent anecdotes refer to children who were at some risk for health or safety because of their habits of mouthing or ingesting inedibles. Parents have found a variety of commonsense and ingenious solutions to this problem.

> When Jim was just a toddler, he moved around very fast and paid no attention to language. He would pick up anything and everything from the floor and put it in his mouth. When we gave him a pacifier and hung it around his neck so that he could always find it, he started to use that instead.

This little boy had clearly developed his motor skills faster than judgment, understanding of language, and memory for rules. The prospect of continuously chasing around behind a fast toddler on the move, or of clearing the whole house or yard of all reachable inedibles, would have been overwhelming. Probably, Jim did not understand why his mother reacted with anger to his impulses and, therefore, punishment would have been counterproductive. Her solution was to provide him with an alternate substance, accepting the fact that he was still at a mouthing stage of development. Another solution based on giving the child an alternate substance to mouth, or in this case to eat, follows:

> My autistic son, Richard, age 4½, loves plants, but in his zeal for them, he eats them. He eats not just one leaf or two, but usually gulps down the whole plant, except the stem. We worried that he could eat the wrong plants but did not want to give up having plants altogether. Verbal reminders not to eat the plants did not work. So on the lower sills we have placed plants of lettuce and herbs. Now he can eat to his heart's content. But now that he is allowed to eat them he has slowed down. I guess the novelty has worn off.

There are two interesting aspects to this ingenious intervention. Richard's mother thought he stopped eating plants because the novelty wore off. From a behavioral point of view, however, we know that she gave frequent attention and reprimands when he bothered her plants. Once she could stop paying attention to his worrisome eating, the main motivation for his behavior was gone. He may have enjoyed a snack now and then, but not as much as he enjoyed her attention.

The second point is that she did not give up her hobby of nurturing house plants. The ability to maintain recreational interests and avocations apart from the handicapped child, or in spite of his or her interfering behaviors, is noted by Bristol (1984) as an important contribution to the mental health and successful adaptation of the family. She points out that parents who continue to give some priority to their own needs have fewer problems with depression and burnout.

The following anecdote illustrates another instance of eating inedibles:

> My son Rick used to eat *all* types of inedible things, (gravel, socks, and so on) until I stopped reacting to it. When he got no reaction from me, he came over to me and said, "I ate string!" Having noticed it was a short piece, I still did not react. Now he has stopped eating inedibles.

This verbal boy's statement, "I ate string," proves to us that Rick wanted his mother to notice and presumably interfere or reprimand. It is less easy to discover reasons for this behavior with nonverbal children who would be more likely to repeat the action, moving closer and closer to mother. Paying no attention to Rick's eating behavior was a most effective way to reduce it. When the substance eaten is dangerous to health or destructive of materials, a different response is called for. The following anecdote illustrates this point:

> When she was 8, my daughter Chita used to chew upholstery or her clothing while watching TV, which she loved. Because she could read, I was able to stop this by writing down the rule "not in your mouth" on a sign just below the TV. Then, when she forgot, I just turned off the set for 1 minute and pointed to the sign.

In this anecdote, we see the use of an immediate aversive response, or punishment (turning off the TV). Chita's mother understood that her daughter was not being intentionally "bad" or manipulative, but rather could not remember to inhibit the impulse. Rather than verbally nag her, and give attention to the actions, she used a written sign placed where she knew her child would be looking. If her daughter had not been able to read, she might have used a picture sign instead. It is impressive that Chita's mother did not stop here.

> However, Chita also ate flowers, grass, and other outdoor plants, and this was dangerous because of the poisons used by our neighboring farmers. I decided to train her ability to inhibit the impulse at a time when she

would be thinking about eating. She loved to chew ice cubes. I placed these in a saucer by her plate with the rule that she must wait until the end of the meal before eating them. She began to echo back the rule "wait," and it seemed to help. The problem didn't disappear, but it did get better. When she could inhibit eating ice throughout the meal, I gave her more freedom outdoors.

Chita's mother recognized her daughter's poor inhibition of impulses. She realized that this self-control needed to be strengthened if the rule "not in your mouth" could be generalized away from the TV. She taught the girl to echo the new rule, "wait," and to practice inhibiting eating something she really wanted that was within reach at the dinner table. When both the awareness of "not in your mouth" and the self-control to "wait" were developed, the mother was willing to give less supervision outdoors.

The next anecdote illustrates the use of an aversive that was immediate and did not require any attention from the parent:

> I was having considerable trouble with my son Elwood (age 8 years), who had a habit of eating the thumbs out of his mittens. After I'd reached the frustration point, my husband suggested I paint the mittens (the places he chewed) with one of those commercially made solutions to stop nail biting. They are clear and don't harm the fabric, but the awful taste has discouraged Elwood's chewing so that his mittens now remain intact and keep his hands warm in the snow and cold.

Picky Eating of Limited Variety

The problem of rigid food preferences, limited variety, and inadequate nutrition is often seen in autistic children. At times, this is only a nuisance and irritant to parents, but it can also result in an unbalanced diet. Over time, this can pose a health hazard. This problem is illustrated by the following example:

> Rami, age 2, refused to eat any solid foods for a long time. I introduced them successfully first by giving him a butter cookie that melted quickly in his mouth. He began to be less fearful and would bite into them by himself. After only 2 weeks he was willing to bite down into other foods as well.

Rami's mother recognized her boy's fear of trying new textures and chose a melting cookie, a sweet taste the boy already enjoyed. She chose a new texture that would naturally disappear soon, thereby avoiding the "spitting out" behavior that might have otherwise resulted. Schroeder and Reese (1984, 1985) point out the need to recognize the child's preferences in terms of color, texture, taste, and smell, in order to successfully introduce new foods. They suggest changing only one aspect at a time—same color, same texture, but new flavor, for example.

In the next anecdote, a child showed a marked preference for the color of foods:

> For a long time, my son Jason would eat only white food: milk, bread, potatoes, cream-of-wheat, yogurt, and so on. I never wanted to make eating unpleasant, and I thought he would grow out of it. But when he was 5 years old, he still maintained this color preference. I used the following technique. I began to add slightly colored ingredients to the white food, very slowly changing the color over a period of many days. I guess he didn't notice these small changes. This technique was effective in getting him to accept a number of different foods.

The very gradual change described is an important aspect of this technique. Jones (1989) and Kozloff (1973) referred to the same gradual change technique. In this case, a boy was given very small amounts of a new food mixed into his favorite, mashed potatoes. Once the new food was accepted more easily, he was willing to take one bite without mixing it, and then was given plain mashed potatoes to follow this one bite. Others have broadened younger children's diet range by rewarding them for trying new food with the immediate delivery of a small portion of their preferred food.

> Joseph, age 6, has always been very fussy about trying anything new. He prefers bread and potatoes (french fries, especially). I got fed up with this one day and tried the following plan. I put the favorite food in a separate dish and a small amount of the other foods on his plate (whatever we were eating). He got a bite of his favorite, then I moved it away and pointed to the other food and waited. Once he put the new food at least in his mouth, I let him have another bite of his favorite. He soon caught on.

There are three interesting aspects to this intervention that are important to note. This parent simply pointed and "waited" but presumably did not nag, thereby giving little attention to the refusals. Second, it was visually clear to Joseph what he could have and when he could have it because his mother used two different dishes. Third, the phrase "at least in his mouth" indicates that complete chewing and swallowing were not required at first. The child was rewarded for any approach to eating different food. The first step in overcoming the fear, or the rigid habit of eating only certain foods, was taken just by placing the food in his mouth. The general principle of "one step at a time" undoubtedly contributed to the success of this intervention.

The next anecdote describes a child who was excessively slow and particular.

> David was a very slow and picky eater when he was 8. We had to prompt him for every mouthful. However, he loved to watch TV, so we placed the TV where he could see it when eating (volume down). Each time he stopped eating (that is, did not take another bite after his mouth was empty for 10 seconds), we turned the set off. He soon learned this consequence, and now we do not have to nag or prompt him through every meal.

In this case, the child was given a continuous reward as long as eating continued. It was a reward that did not interrupt the family meal. Kozloff (1973) gave an example of a similar continuous reward technique, although in his report the parent talked to the child in a pleasant way as long as he continued to eat, turning away when he stopped. Stiver and Dobbins (1980) also used a continuous reward technique with an 11-year-old autistic girl who showed potential anorexia, a severe onset of food refusal. She was allowed to stay in the large school cafeteria, which she enjoyed, only if she ate. Her mother was advised to stop all discussion of eating in front of the girl. The importance of giving less verbal attention to eating problems is mentioned by Holmes (1982). He found that a 5½-year-old boy's eating improved during the 3 weeks that his parents were taking a baseline measure, simply recording what he did eat with no intervention at all. These parents reported that they altered their feeding expectations and behaviors as they acquired a better understanding of their child's feeding patterns.

Withholding snacks, especially junk foods, is a commonsense measure, but this is not always easy with an autistic child who can climb up to shelves and open the refrigerator.

> My daughter Sara, age 5, never wanted to eat a balanced meal. She only wanted to eat junk foods, such as potato chips, cookies, candy, and soda. One day I kept it all out of sight and cooked a balanced meal. Around 4 P.M. she was so hungry she asked for food, and I gave her a balanced meal. She has been eating ever since.

Keeping all snacks out of sight is an important aspect of this technique. This mother's organized structuring of her meal time was of great help, since Sara was not constantly tempted to eat and was dependent on her mother for food. She was able to experience hunger, which helped her to accept the regular meal. The resulting improvement in nutrition could lead to better health and improved behavior. White (1982) reported withholding snacks for 3 hours before meals with a 13-year-old boy. He also allowed the boy to come to the family table for dessert only after he had finished the first course at a separate table. Withholding food is not comfortable for many parents of handicapped children. But when the food withheld is actually harmful to their health, there is no conflict.

> My 12-year-old son, Bruce, has been hyperactive with temper tantrums. He was on Mellaril, but I wanted to reduce this medication. I began using all natural foods and substituted Listerine for toothpaste. I used bottled water and diluted most beverages with this. I eliminated pork as well as grape and cherry Kool-Aid, which I discovered made him much more hyperactive. I have seen a real difference in his behavior.

Specific allergies and sensitivity to sugar and food coloring are reported by a number of parents. Bruce's mother used her observations to test her dietary hypothesis by modifying his diet, and thus was able to find that limiting specific foods improved his behavior.

Overeating

In contrast to the picky eater is the child who seems to be always hungry, who eats too much but is not satisfied. The next two anecdotes report original solutions to this problem.

Our Janice is very large for her age (10 years) and likes to eat a tremendous amount of food. Her main occupation at home, when not distracted by something else, is raiding the refrigerator. This results in constant spills and messes, not to mention overeating. We tried teaching her to stay away from the refrigerator, but this didn't work if we were out of sight. Luckily ours has two doors (freezer and fridge, side by side), so we bought a plastic lock and locked the doors together. She has not figured out how to unlock the padlock and so leaves the food alone.

Although this autistic girl was 10 years old, it is apparent from this description that she did not understand language and had not developed inhibition of her impulse to eat when no one was there. This mother wisely understood that she needed to rearrange the environment to adapt to the child's handicap, making overeating physically impossible. The importance of the child's health is obvious, but the importance of the sanity of the whole family should also be recognized. The next anecdote describes the same problem, but with a boy who has more understanding of rules and consequences.

My autistic son, Tod (12 years old), always seems to be hungry; he never gets full no matter how much I give him. His weight became a problem, so I had to deny him third helpings. He doesn't understand language, so I kept just enough for a second helping in the pan and then let him see as I scraped out all that was left. He could then understand that there was no more. His anger is not a problem now that he understands why I don't give him more.

The impressive lesson in this anecdote is that Tod's mother understood that his anger was related to not being able to understand why he was denied food. She realized that she could not control his unusual appetite but could control the amount he ate. She found a visual way to explain this rule thus bypassing the language handicap.

Eating Behavior

Appropriate behavior during meals is learned gradually by all children. Most parents find that they can teach their children through verbal explanations and demonstration. This is not always possible with autistic children. Eating too fast, excessive messing and playing with food, and stealing food from others' plates also are problems with adults and older retarded children in institutions. Some researchers (Azrin & Armstrong, 1973; Hendriksen & Doughty, 1967) reported using continuous behavior shaping during meals to reward appropriate eating behavior and interrupt inappropriate behavior. Some have pointed out the need to interrupt food stealing before it can be completed because the food is such a strong reward in itself. In this case, the adult "shadowed" the child's arm and redirected him to a more appropriate eating behavior before the food stealing could be completed. Others (Groves & Carroscio, 1971; Kozloff, 1974) have used brief withdrawal of the food to point out to children the behaviors that were unacceptable, or removed the food for 10 seconds following each mistake. These researchers used praise and some manual prompts to encourage all appropriate behaviors. The same training techniques can be seen in the following anecdotes.

> Shad, age 6½, always ate in a hurry. He used his left hand to shovel food into his mouth and constantly needed to be reminded to use only one hand. By putting a napkin in his left hand, we eliminated this mealtime problem. It worked immediately. Meals are a lot less frustrating now.

Since verbal reminders were not effective, this mother recognized that her son was not able to organize and control the movement of both of his hands—his left hand was moving impulsively. She interrupted this behavior by giving his left hand something to hold, an alternate action. The next parent also reports having no success with verbal reprimands.

> Jack, age 7, really loves food. He shovels it in faster than he can chew and swallow. We tried scolding him, but he did not understand what was wrong and just got mad. So I made a large red stop sign out of cardboard (he does know what this means) and placed it over his plate as soon as he took one bite. I removed it after he had swallowed what was in his mouth. He soon caught on, and now I only have to use the stop sign when he forgets to chew and swallow what's in his mouth.

Here the "shoveling" behavior is prevented by the cardboard sign, which is a visual reminder (a symbol Jack understands) to increase appropriate inhibition and permit chewing and swallowing to occur naturally.

One mother records her effort to keep her child at the meal table by removing her daughter's food if she leaves.

Sally, age 5, was always on the go; she wouldn't sit still for anything for long. She used to take a bite at mealtimes and then be off and away, coming back for another bite, and so on. Scolding was unpleasant for the whole family, ruining meals. I began by making a big display at the end of our meals, saying "I'm finished" and taking my plate to the sink. I did the same with others as soon as they got up, saying "Oh, you're finished." Then I started to do the same with her plate as soon as she got up. She looked horrified and very unhappy. But this worked.

Sally's mother realized that verbal warnings were not going to prepare her for the consequence of leaving the table. However, she did prepare Sally for the event by demonstrating the rule "when you are finished, your plate is removed" with the other members of the family. Although it came as a shock to Sally, it was not an unfamiliar routine and was therefore easy to understand. Sally was quick to learn that she must stay with the family at mealtime.

A child's unwillingness to swallow pills is a problem both for doctors prescribing medications and for parents who must make their children take pills. The following anecdotes describe one family's success with twin autistic boys.

In the beginning, I taught John to take a pill in the following way: Holding one of his hands, I gave him the pill and demonstrated or pointed to get him to put it in his mouth. Then *quickly* I placed a glass of water in his free hand and told him to take a drink. He had not yet mastered spitting things out, so it worked very well. Now in getting John and David to take their pills we have come up with an interesting technique. Mother, father, daughter, and the boys sit in a circle each with a pill and a glass of water. One by one we take (or fake taking) a pill, going around the circle until we get to the boys. Most often they will follow right along and imitate our taking the pills.

Here again we see a whole family structuring a routine in order to help their autistic child understand what is required. This is a fine illustration of family cooperation and caring to help the member with a handicap. The initial individual training that preceded this technique was important to its success. Manual assistance, gestural prompts, and one familiar verbal phrase, "Take a drink," enabled this boy to get through the whole procedure quickly before he had time to get upset about the pill itself.

The last anecdote in this section pertains to the behavior of not attempting to feed at all. Some autistic children remain passive and dependent even after their motor skills are sufficient for self-feeding. In response to this passivity and fear that their child may go hungry, most parents find themselves spoon-feeding the child. This parent chose to do otherwise:

> Our daughter Sulin, age 28 months, made no effort to feed herself. I stood behind her highchair and manipulated her arms like a puppet. Slowly I began fading these prompts (just touching her hands, then just her forearms, and so on) as she began to take over. This was successful.

Leibowitz and Holler (1974) used a similar technique with a 5-year-old girl who was not using a spoon and was very limited in what she would accept. They began using a spoon for ice cream, her favorite, so that she would be highly motivated to get this substance to her mouth. Gradually other items were mixed with the ice cream. In less than a month, this girl was using a spoon herself and accepting new foods.

Rumination and Vomiting

These disturbing behaviors that can follow eating were not mentioned by the parents contributing to this collection. However, these behaviors do exist, and several reports of successful behavioral interventions can be found in the literature for those who are interested. These reports vary in their procedures, using aversives, stimulus control, rewards, training of alternate behaviors, or a combination of these (Ball, Hendrickson & Clarton, 1974; Borreson & Anderson, 1982; Daniel, 1982; Schroeder, 1989; Singh, Manning, & Angell, 1982).

One study (Daniel, 1982) stopped rumination in a 10-year-old retarded boy by promoting walking at the time he usually ruminated. This was an incompatible behavior; that is, this child did not ruminate when he was actively walking. Gradually the behavior disappeared. Another intervention study (Mulick, Schroeder, & Rojahn, 1980) tried several behavioral techniques before concluding that reinforcement of alternate behaviors after the meal was the most successful in reducing ruminative vomiting. A third (Murray, Keele, & McCarver, 1977) eliminated vomiting in a 5-year-old male who was hospitalized for malnutrition from vomiting. The child's food was thickened, making regurgitation more difficult. They held and supported the child during feedings and for 20 minutes afterward. If ruminating started, the child was put down and a drop of hot sauce was placed on his tongue. He was picked up again and rocked as soon as the first sign of the behavior (tongue rolling) ceased. All vomiting ceased in 2 weeks. Another technique was used with 17-year-old twins who had been ruminating since age 6 (Singh et al., 1982). When either of them started, they were reprimanded ("no") and required to clean their teeth for 2 minutes with a toothbrush soaked in mouthwash and then wipe their lips with a cloth dipped in mouthwash. This stopped the ruminating and prevented further damage to the lining of their esophagus and mouth.

SLEEPING

It will come as no surprise that none of the collected anecdotes pertains to children who sleep too much. Some developmentally handicapped children seem to survive easily and remain healthy with less sleep than other children their age. It is the parents' health, both mental and physical, that one worries about. Sleep deprivation is physically exhausting and places great stress on all family relationships. Some parents find themselves driven to punitive responses they themselves do not approve of. Others sometimes seek out relief by giving their child medications. The following anecdotes offer creative examples and hope to those parents who suffer from lack of sleep and worry over their child's safety. The anecdotes are arranged by groups according to when the problem occurs: children who will not go to sleep, children who wake up and wander, and children who have problems in the morning in relation to sleep patterns.

Problem Going to Sleep

When Larry was young, he would not sleep in his bed. Since he liked to rock and liked music, I put a rocking chair and music in his room. He was allowed to listen to this until he became sleepy. Slowly he learned to transition himself to the bed as he grew drowsy.

This mother provided her son with an environment she knew would be pleasant and relaxing for him. She put no pressure on him but let his body become naturally drowsy in its own time. In this relaxed state, he was able to accept being moved to his bed and eventually could make this transition himself without her prompts.

> Our daughter Barbara, age 9, used to have great difficulty sleeping. We purchased an artificial noise maker—water sounds—and installed it in her closet. This sound covered the other household noises and allowed her to sleep through most disturbances. Also, she slept much better after her room was insulated and we placed carpeting on the floor and on one wall.

Hypersensitivity to sounds, especially those outside the room where the child is, is a familiar characteristic of autistic children. They may act deaf to sounds near them, especially to language, yet be overalert to distant sounds. Barbara's mother clearly recognized this characteristic in her child and saw that it was interrupting the child's natural sleep patterns. Other parents have reported using records, tapes, and radio music to screen out household sounds that interrupt sleeping. The next anecdote describes a young child who could stay in bed, but would not accept any covers.

> Our autistic daughter, Pat, age 5, refused to accept being covered by blankets. We had to wait until she fell asleep before covering her. If she woke, she would throw her blankets on the floor. To get her to accept blankets, we covered her dolls with blankets and said, "Dolly is going to bed." After a few nights she covered her dolls herself, and she also began to accept being covered with blankets.

Rather than have a battle at bedtime, which is seldom conducive to the state of drowsiness, these parents used a doll-play technique to teach their daughter the appropriate behavior at bedtime. By repeating the play for several nights, they were able to introduce her to this new routine in a nonpunitive, gentle manner.

The next anecdote describes Mary, who resisted going to bed and who was not able to understand rules or inhibit behaviors. We see how the technique of physical containment eventually worked over a period of time.

When our autistic daughter outgrew her crib, bedtime became a nightmare. Not only did Mary refuse to stay in bed, she wouldn't stay in her room. Our pediatrician suggested lowering the light, closing the door, and leaving her alone. Although the room was as childproof as we could make it, Mary had no sense of danger. We were concerned for her safety and not comfortable putting her behind a closed door. Our simple solution for several years was to stretch a wooden baby gate across the door. The entire room was treated as her bed. Mary was not a climber and never made an effort to get out. She would stand behind the gate able to hear and see normal household functions. As she wound down and grew drowsy, she almost always made her way to her bed and would fall asleep. Occasionally, we found her asleep on the carpeted floor. She slept in a "blanket" sleeper instead of pajamas, so we never worried about having to cover her. As Mary got older, she still resisted bedtime. She also become too strong for the wooden gate we had used, so we replaced it with a Dutch door—my husband's ingenious invention. He sawed an old wooden door in half. The glass panels on the top half were replaced with unbreakable plexiglass. When the top half of the door is closed to keep out the noise, we can still view Mary's activities inside the room through the glass panels. Routinely, however, only the bottom half is closed, and it confines her to the bedroom. As Mary grows older, there are now nights when she is less hyperactive, and she is able to stay in bed with the door left entirely open. But the Dutch door is there if we need it, and it has proved to be a workable solution for all of us over the years.

As we view hyperactive Mary at the younger age, we can easily understand how bedtime could become a nightmare. By their ingenious way of adapting the environment to protect their daughter, these parents eliminated their worries and annoyances. This family was able to survive the severe sleeping difficulty Mary presented and maintain her in their home until the hyperactivity began to lessen with age and the problem disappeared.

Nighttime Wandering

The following anecdotes concern the problem of waking in the middle of the night and roaming around the house.

Josh, age 4, kept getting up at night and wandering. He was safe in his
room, but not in the rest of the house. My husband took the door handle
off and turned it around so that it would lock on the outside and not on
the inside of his room.

The familiar saying "An ounce of prevention is worth a pound of
cure" comes to mind with this anecdote. The success of this solution
depended on the stated fact that Josh "was safe in his room." This is
not always the case, as we see in the next anecdote.

Our daughter Sandy, age 5, wouldn't sleep, and she wandered around the
house at night. For a few nights I slept on the floor outside of her room.
This prevented her from leaving her room and made her feel safe.
Gradually, I moved farther away from her door until I was able to sleep
in my own room and she learned to stay in her room.

Sandy's mother was more concerned about her daughter's emotional safety than her physical safety. She recognized Sandy's wakeful
wandering as a search for her mother because of a feeling of insecurity
or loneliness and felt this was legitimate. She interrupted the wandering
by her physical presence at the doorway, and then gradually withdrew
to increasing distances as her daughter gained confidence and could
manage alone. By this technique, she avoided initiating a routine of
having Sandy come into the parents' bed, which could have developed
into a ritual that would be difficult to change. Although all young
children go through periods of night wakefulness and have need for
comfort after bad dreams, autistic children often get stuck in habits
after the genuine need has passed.

Many parents have reported feeling uncomfortable with the idea of
preventing their child from leaving his or her room. They worry about
possible dangers from fire or other hazards. However, children sometimes wander without being fully conscious of what they are doing.
They may have their eyes wide open and be able to maneuver safely
around the house, but have no memory of what they have done, and
little judgment.

My son, Ramon, age 6, went through a period of nightwalking, or
sleepwalking. He seemed awake, but remembered nothing in the morn-

ing. We placed a large armchair in Ramon's doorway at night. He could get out by sliding between the chair and the doorway, but it was just difficult enough to wake him up. Usually, he went back to bed again.

This solution is a form of partial containment. The barricade is not total, and the child can get out of the room if he really needs to. However, it served to wake him up. Other parents have used similar techniques, such as a heavy rope at waist level, or a small gate that can be climbed over or crawled under if needed. The next anecdote concerns a boy who was safe in his room and safe in the house at night, but who learned how to open the front door.

> Daryl has always been a restless sleeper and night wanderer, but he stayed in the house and did not cause any trouble. However, when he began to leave the house to "go get the paper" at night, something had to be done. Daryl soon learned to undo the lock and slide out the chain. So we padlocked the chain in such a way that it would no longer reach the opening. This kept him from opening the door and solved the problem.

Morning Sleep Problems

Two different morning problems are addressed in the following anecdotes—the child who wakes up too early and is ready to go and the child who does not wake up early enough for school.

> By the age of 8, Brian knew he had to get up each morning at 7:00. He would get up several times from 5:30 on, and run through the house to check the digital clock to see if it was 7:00 yet. This also woke up the other members of the family. I put a digital stick-up clock on the headboard of Brian's bed. He then checked the time without running all through the house disturbing the other family members.

Brian had already mastered two important skills or abilities: He could read a digital clock, and he had developed social awareness in respecting rules and the self-control to follow them. All that was missing was having the information about time. These parents found an original way to supply this information in his room, thus solving the problem. The final anecdote presents the opposite problem—the child does not wake up early enough.

John had difficulty waking up on time to get ready for school. If awakened by us, he was usually in a very bad mood. I discovered that if I let his pet cat into the house, the cat would go and jump on his bed, nuzzle up to his face, and pester him until he woke up—in a *good* mood.

This ingenious solution was possible, not only because John liked his cat, but because his parents were good observers and sensitive to his interests and preferences.

The problem of not waking easily or in a good mood can come from various causes. Children who have trouble falling asleep may be allowed to stay up as late as they want and, therefore, are in need of more sleep when it's time for them to get ready for school. Some children may experience unusually deep sleep in the early morning regardless of when they went to bed. A third reason may be a "hangover" effect from having taken medication. We have not discussed the use of medication in this chapter, although it can be helpful with some children for a certain period of time. A doctor who is familiar with autistic children and their reaction to specific medications should be consulted. Dalldorf (1985), Paluszny (1979), and Ritvo (1976) all report the temporary, carefully monitored use of sedatives that may be effective in changing sleep patterns for one child but not the next. Medication is used only after other methods have failed. Dalldorf (1985) suggests checking out the following points before discussing medication with your doctor. Is the child given adequate and predictable bedtime routines and schedules? Does he or she get sufficient exercise? Is the child getting caffeine beverages in the evening or other stimulating foods such as sugar or chocolate? If sleep is frequently interrupted, does the child have chronic nasal obstructions? Are the sleep arrangements too noisy for this child?

If sleep disturbances continue after common causes such as these are ruled out, medication may be temporarily helpful. However, data should be taken on the hours the child goes to bed, goes to sleep, and wakes up. The doctor supervising the medication should also know what behavioral techniques have been tried and their effectiveness. After medication disrupts the habituated sleeplessness, preventive methods such as illustrated in the preceding anecdotes are likely to become effective.

REFERENCES

Azrin, N. H., & Armstrong, P. M. (1973). The mini-meal: A method for teaching eating skills to the profoundly retarded. *Mental Retardation, 11*(1), 9–13.

Ball, T. S., Hendrickson, H., & Clarton, J. (1974). A special feeding technique for chronic regurgitation. *American Journal of Mental Deficiency, 78,* 486–493.

Borreson, P. M., & Anderson, J. L. (1982). The elimination of chronic rumination through a combination of procedures. *Mental Retardation, 20*(1), 34–38.

Brazelton, T. B. (1974). *Toddlers and parents.* New York: Dell.

Bristol, M. M. (1984). Family resources and successful adaptation to autistic children. In E. Schopler & G. B. Mesibov (Eds.), *The effects of autism on the family* (pp. 289–310). New York: Plenum Press.

Dalldorf, J. S. (1985). *Medical aspects of the autism syndrome* [Unpublished Monograph]. Chapel Hill: University of North Carolina at Chapel Hill, Medical School, Division TEACCH.

Daniel, W. H. (1982). A management of chronic rumination with contingent exercise employing topographically dissimilar behavior. *Journal of Behavioral Therapy and Experimental Psychiatry, 13,* 149–152.

Groves, I. D., & Carroscio, D. F. (1971). A self-feeding program for the severely and profoundly retarded. *Mental Retardation, 9*(3), 10–13.

Hendriksen, K., & Doughty, R. (1967). Decelerating undesired mealtime behavior in a group of profoundly retarded boys. *American Journal of Mental Deficiency, 72,* 40–44.

Holmes, C. A. (1982). Self-monitoring reactivity and a severe feeding problem. *Journal of Clinical Child Psychology, 11,* 66–71.

Jones, T. W. (1989). Behavior related eating disorders. In *Treatment of psychiatric disorders* (pp. 57–67). Washington, DC: American Psychiatric Association.

Kozloff, M. A. (1973). *Reaching the autistic child.* Champaign, IL: Research Press.

Kozloff, M. A. (1974). *Educating children with learning and behavior problems.* New York: Wiley and Sons.

Leibowitz, J. M., & Holler, P. (1974). Building and maintaining self-feeding skills in a retarded child. *Journal of Occupational Therapy, 28,* 545–548.

Mulick, J. A., Schroeder, S. R., & Rojahn, J. (1980). Chronic ruminative vomiting: A comparison of four treatment procedures. *Journal of Autism and Developmental Disorders, 10,* 203–214.

Murray, M. E., Keele, D. K., & McCarver, J. W. (1977). Treatment of ruminations with behavioral techniques: A case report. *Journal of Behavior Therapy, 8,* 999–1003.

Paluszny, M. D. (1979). *Autism: A practical guide for parents and professionals.* New York: Syracuse University Press.

Ritvo, E. R. (Ed.). (1976). *Autism: Diagnosis, current research and management.* New York: Spectrum.

Schroeder, S. R. (1989). Rumination. In *Treatments of psychiatric disorders* (Vol. 1, pp. 53–55). Washington, DC: American Psychiatric Association.

Schroeder, S. R., & Reese, M. (1984/1985, Spring Semester). Picky eating and stimulus control: A research project. *TEACCHer's report.* Chapel Hill, NC: University of North Carolina, Division TEACCH.

Singh, N. N., Manning, D. J., & Angell, M. J. (1982). Effects of oral hygiene punishment procedure on chronic rumination and collateral behaviors in monozygous twins. *Journal of Applied Behavior Analysis, 15,* 302–314.

Spock, B., & Rothenberg, M. B. (1985). Dr. Spock's baby and child care. New York: Simon & Schuster.

Stiver, R. L., & Dobbins, J. P. (1980). Treatment of atypical anorexia nervosa in the public school: An autistic girl. *Journal of Autism and Developmental Disorders, 10,* 67–74.

White, A. J. (1982). Outpatient treatment of oppositional non-eating in a deaf retarded boy. *Journal of Behavior Therapy and Experimental Psychiatry, 13,* 251–255.

8

Behavior Management

Problem Behaviors

Underlying Deficits

A mong the problems of child rearing, concerns with behavior management preoccupy most parents at one time or another, whether or not their child has autism. The unique problems of autism, including communication deficits, inappropriate social interaction, and narrow interests, pose behavioral challenges for all concerned. Parents, teachers, and caretakers typically find their experience with siblings and other children of little help. Instead, parents have to learn from living with their child and making use of that experience. Sometimes they also get help from knowledgeable professionals familiar with many such children and behavioral research. From that experience, they often learn that the most enduring and effective way to overcome these behavior problems is to understand the child's special needs and find out what sets off the behavior. On the basis of that information, parents, teachers, or caregivers may then teach the child a compensating skill or alter the environment to accommodate the underlying deficit. Both approaches can neutralize undesirable behaviors.

Improving the individual's skills and accommodating the environment to the blocking deficit are two teaching priorities that have been implemented in our 30 years of parent–professional collaboration in Division TEACCH (Mesibov, in press). From our experience, we have given special emphasis to the prevention of behavior problems through structured teaching and modification of undesirable behavior through a process represented by the iceberg metaphor discussed previously.

In the preceding chapters, we showed how anecdotes of effective coping can be understood best through the procedures represented by use of that same iceberg metaphor. In this chapter, we review behavior management principles relating to the development of new skills or environmental modification, and we identify links with the concepts and principles of formal behavioral research (Schreibman, 1994). A number of anecdotes are included to show how parents sometimes spontaneously use principles from behavioral research. In many cases, these were not taught, but were learned from observation of their own child. In our experience, the vast majority of behavior problems can be prevented or resolved through compensatory skills and environmental accommodation. A small proportion of behavior problems, usually severe with a long reinforcement history, cannot be resolved by understanding the underlying trigger mechanism, which remains unknown despite our best information and efforts. In such cases, the principles of classic operant conditioning may be invoked. This technique involves the conditioning of a specific response—increasing it with rewards and decreasing it with punishment—without attention to the whole person.

GENERAL BEHAVIOR MANAGEMENT PRINCIPLES

In general, the behavior management principles commonly used in special education settings involve manipulating the consequences of a specific behavior in order to modify that behavior (Ruggles & LeBlanc, 1985). This is based on the assumption that the child is engaging in a behavior in order to achieve a specific result. The frequency with which the child displays that behavior can be controlled by decreasing or increasing the frequency with which the child achieves the desired result. *Reinforcement* increases the chance of a behavior occurring. *Punishment* is the term professionals use for procedures that decrease the chance of a behavior occurring. In the following sections, a variety of positive reinforcement procedures will be described, since the most effective behavior changes occur when a predominance of positive reinforcement is used.

Positive reinforcement is a general term that stands for an object or event that strengthens a behavior when it follows that behavior (Kanoly & Rosenthal, 1977). The purpose of positive reinforcement is to increase the frequency or duration of a given behavior. Positive reinforcement can be given in a variety of ways: a smile, physical affection, a food reward, a compliment, and so on. Each of us uses positive reinforcement all the time, whether or not we are aware of it. Reinforcement is most successful if it regularly and predictably follows a given behavior. Parents sometimes find that using positive reinforcement with autistic children is difficult, since it is often hard to find something that is interesting to their child. In other words, for a reward to be successful, the child must want it enough so that he or she will do what you want in order to get that reward. For example, saying "Good boy, Danny" may be effective for many 5-year-olds, but may have a limited effect on the behavior of an autistic child. It is also important that children understand clearly that they must perform a specific behavior in order to get the reward they want.

Token System

In a token system, the child is given a token (such as money, checks, or stars) after he or she performs an appropriate behavior (Fjellstedt & Sulzer-Azaroff, 1973). These tokens are later turned in for something the child wants, such as foods, toys, or an activity he or she likes. Tokens are successful only for children who are capable of understanding that they will receive what they want at a later time. Some children are not able to understand this delay and need immediate reinforcement after they perform a given behavior. One feature of tokens is that they can be given for good behavior and taken away or withheld for bad behavior. A parent described how she used a token system to improve her daughter's behavior:

> My daughter Marcie, age 17, has sporadic episodes of bad behavior on her school bus. After talking to her bus driver and teacher, we decided to send in a slip of paper on which the bus driver records whether she has good, so-so, or bad behavior. For good behavior she earns one cent; for so-so behavior she gets nothing; and for bad behavior she loses one cent. She is able to cash the money in for things she likes at school and at home. Since we began this system, her behavior has improved dramatically, as she is generally able to earn her money.

Marcie's bad behavior on the school bus was potentially dangerous. It was difficult for the driver to give her positive reinforcement while driving. Therefore, Marcie's mother and teacher set up a token system for her to earn or lose money according to her behavior on the bus. This system reduced her misbehavior and enabled her to earn some money. It is important to note that Marcie was capable of understanding that the marks on the paper were connected to the rewards she would get later on. Without this understanding, a token system would not have been possible.

Differential Reinforcement of Behavior

Differential reinforcement of other behavior (DRO) is a technical term that means giving positive reinforcement when an inappropriate behavior does not occur. For example, for a child who likes to spit, a teacher may set a timer and give the child a reward if he didn't spit while the timer was running. Researchers have found that this method of treatment has been just as effective as mild punishment in getting rid of inappropriate behavior (Haring & Kennedy, 1990; Sulzer-Azaroff & Pollack, 1985). Another advantage of this approach is that it generally strengthens desired behavior, such as on-task behavior. A parent gave an example of how she used this approach to eliminate a troublesome behavior of her son:

> When Bob was 3, he liked to play in our backyard, but came into the house frequently. Every time he went in and out, he let the screen door bang shut. No matter how often I told him not to slam the door, he ignored me. One day, for whatever reason, the door didn't slam after he came in. I praised him, gave him a cookie, and hugged him. Since then, simple as it sounds, I've learned that ignoring the "bad" behavior and praising "good" things (no matter how long I have to wait for the "good" things) is a quicker and more long-lasting solution.

Bob's mother had the good fortune of accidently discovering an effective way to eliminate a bothersome behavior. Her verbal reprimands for slamming the door were ineffective. Once she praised him for not slamming the door, he quickly learned that it was worth it not to slam the door, because he would get a reward. Troublesome behavior was eliminated by rewarding good behavior rather than punishing bad behavior.

Extinction

Extinction is a technical term for something that we all do to other people—decrease the occurrence of a behavior by withholding the reinforcer for that behavior (Ruggles & LeBlanc, 1985). For example, a tired mother who sits down to read the evening paper may be nagged by her husband. Rather than saying "Yes, dear," she finds that he will leave her alone if she ignores him. Similarly, teachers often find that if they pay no attention to an inappropriate behavior, it may go away. For this procedure to be effective, it is important to recognize what the child wants to get out of a given behavior. Given the unusual interests that some autistic children display, parents may find that their child is seeking unique reinforcers.

> When Jon was 6, he used to love to turn certain switches on and off. He would open the refrigerator door and manually push the light button over and over. We simply took out the bulb. Jon would also turn our TV on and off. By adjusting the "bright" knob, we could make the TV screen totally dark. This discouraged Jon from turning the TV on and off.

In Jon's case, his parents were able to assess what he found fascinating about playing with the TV or the refrigerator lights. Their solution was simple—to remove the "fun" consequences of switching those appliances; that is, they changed the environment. This eliminated Jon's habit of playing with these appliances and allowed him to be more independent in the home without being destructive to property.

Response Cost

Another procedure designed to decrease a particular behavior is called *response cost*. This technique involves taking away something that the child finds reinforcing when he or she displays a particular behavior (Weiner, 1962). Because something is being taken away, this is a mild form of punishment. Response cost is very direct and clear to the child, and is generally effective whenever the reinforcer is strong enough. One parent relates how she used such a treatment for her son's grabbing behavior:

> My 15-year-old son, Kevin, has a tendency to grab people whenever he can't get his way. He likes TV and radio very much. Whenever he starts his grabbing act, we turn off the TV and tell him that he is not allowed to play the radio either. After doing this a few times, we found that whenever he started grabbing, we could remind him that we were going

to turn off the TV; he would then calm down immediately. Over time, his grabbing behavior became much less frequent.

These parents used a mild punishment for their son's grabbing behavior, taking away something he liked. This direct cause-and-effect procedure, "grab and you lose the TV," made sense to Kevin and helped him to control his grabbing.

Differential Reinforcement of Incompatible Behaviors

In dealing with inappropriate behaviors, it is important to avoid confrontations whenever possible. One way to avoid confrontations is to suggest alternative behaviors, particularly those that are incompatible with the inappropriate behavior. For example, for a child who likes to flap his hands, you may suggest that he put his hands in his pockets. A father described his solution to a common problem:

> My teenage son Tom likes to rock back and forth. He will do this in any kind of chair and does not seem to be aware if he is bothering other people. Instead of punishing him, I tell him to put his feet together. This makes it difficult for him to rock. Whenever I see him sitting with his feet together, I praise him.

This father did two things to improve his son's behavior. First, he suggested an alternative behavior that made it hard for Tom to rock. Second, he rewarded him for the more appropriate behavior. This combination of methods can be powerful for eliminating undesirable behaviors and teaching new ones.

Time Out

Time out involves temporarily removing a child from ongoing activities in response to some undesired behavior (Ruggles & LeBlanc, 1985; Schreibman, 1994). This can be done in various ways, such as removing the child from a given room or isolating the child within a room by having him or her sit in the corner. For time out to be effective, there must be something reinforcing in the situation that the child is removed from. Generally, time out is used when the child's undesirable behavior is maintained by the attention received in the room, even through some form of reprimand. It is important that time out be used for a set period of time, usually of short duration or no more than a few minutes. Parents have used time-out procedures in a variety of ways.

When my son George was around 10, his teachers used a time-out booth to help control his inappropriate behaviors. At first, I set up a time-out booth in his bedroom closet, which had a lighting switch that he could not control. I was uncomfortable with this, faded it out, and began to use his bedroom as a preferred time-out space. I reversed the lock on his bedroom door and put a timer outside the door. Later, I was able to set the timer on the stove and no longer had to lock the door. George was able to control the door and learned not to come out of the room until the timer went off. Time out has always helped to calm him when he is agitated and served as an effective warning when he started getting wild.

Mike, age 8, loved to follow his two teenage sisters and their friends into their room and listen to records. The girls wanted to include him, but became upset when he began his destructive behavior. We made a deal that he could go in with them, but at the first indication of bad behavior, he had to leave. We were very firm about this, and after a while, it really began to work. He enjoyed the music, and the girls were happy that his behavior was good and that they could help take care of him.

Although time out was used differently for George and Mike, it was an effective way to control their behavior. In George's case, his mother had to cut him off from the rest of the home for a set period of time. This helped him to calm down and enabled his mother to control him without having to get involved in a power struggle. In Mike's case, this procedure was more of a social time out in that Mike was removed from a social situation that he wanted to be part of. His desire to be with his sisters and their friends was strong enough to motivate him to control himself when he was in their room.

Social Disapproval

Social disapproval is a common parenting technique used by parents of all of children (Doleys, Wells, Hobbs, Roberts, & Cartelli, 1976). Disapproval is expressed either verbally (that is, by asking someone not to do something) or by facial expression. For children with autism, social disapproval is most effective with those functioning at a high enough level to be able to understand such communication. Although social disapproval can eliminate inappropriate behavior, it does not in itself teach the child a more positive replacement behavior. Nevertheless, sometimes social disapproval is effective in suppressing undesirable behavior without immediate replacement of constructive substitute behavior.

> Our son Jack, who is 12 years old, has the bad habit of pulling on people's sleeves. Sometimes when he does this, I tell him, "You can't be with us unless you can behave," and send him to another room. When he does this at school, the teachers say "No!" and turn their backs on him. He pulls on people much less frequently now than he used to.

These parents and teachers expressed their disapproval of Jack's behavior by giving him a verbal reprimand. The reprimands were carried out consistently at home and at school, which helped him reduce the "pulling" behavior. It is important to look at a child's negative behavior and ask what may be motivating the child to do it. In this case, Jack may have been trying to communicate to his parents but may not have had the needed communication skills. It is possible that when he first started the sleeve pulling, if another signal for gaining the adult's attention had been taught, this operant conditioning technique might have been unnecessary.

Another parent described a less direct form of social disapproval effective with her grandson:

> My autistic grandson, Tom, now 17, wants very much to be grown up. He was very proud when he was able to attend senior high school. When he behaves childishly, we tell him, "Big men who attend high school do not behave like a little guy." When eating, if he doesn't want to eat something that is good for him, we tell him, "This kind of food helps you to be a big, tall man." This has worked for over a year now.

Tom's grandparents used a subtle form of social disapproval, motivating him to behave better by encouraging him to grow up. This strategy was successful for two reasons: Tom was able enough to understand what it meant to behave more like a grown-up, and his grandparents capitalized on his desire to attend high school and to see himself becoming more adult.

Teaching a New Behavior

Other chapters of this book contain examples of decreasing behavior problems by teaching a new communication skill. There are some instances when a new behavior can be taught as a way of working around a behavior problem. This can be an effective and long-lasting means of dissolving troublesome behavior. One parent reported using this way of coping with her son's potentially dangerous behavior:

> When John was 10, we worried constantly that he'd wander off. We live on a farm and could not trust John out of our sight. Often he did not answer when we called him. We noticed he was attracted to a bicycle horn we gave him. He loved it and hauled it along everywhere with him the whole summer. We became weary of hearing the honking, but we always knew where he was while he was outside. When it was quiet too long, we would shout loudly, "John, honk!" He was delighted to respond by honking his horn.

This anecdote is an admirable example of solving a behavior problem with a positive approach. John's parents were naturally fearful that his wandering off could cause trouble. Instead of punishing him or revoking his privilege of being outside, they taught him to honk his horn. This allowed him to roam around the farm, and at the same time provided him with a way of identifying his whereabouts even though he was nonverbal.

Another common problem is how to prevent children from embarrassing their parents with odd behavior in public. One mother offered an interesting solution:

> My 17-year-old son, Sammy, is a high-level adolescent. When we go shopping, it is necessary for me to take Sammy and his two brothers. All of the children tend to become bored during the shopping. I collected a number of coupons, which I give to each of the children including Sammy. Sammy's task is to look throughout the store and find the item that matches his coupon. This keeps him occupied and happy and makes shopping an educational experience for him.

Sammy's mother offered a creative solution to the common problem of embarrassment during a shopping trip. She taught Sammy a new skill, reading coupons and finding the correct item, and prevented his misbehaving due to boredom. This type of positive approach has the advantage of preventing a behavior problem, teaching a new skill, and helping with shopping all at the same time.

Altering the Environment

There are times when it is difficult to stop an undesirable behavior or to replace it with a constructive one. Under these conditions, some parents find it more convenient and less disruptive to all concerned if they modify their home environment in order to prevent the behavior. This is illustrated in the next two anecdotes.

> My 11-year-old daughter, Tammy, had the habit of turning over furniture. Whenever she was left alone in a room, the furniture ended up upside-down. To prevent her from doing this, we nailed some of the furniture into the wall. We also purchased mostly brass and wood furniture, since this was harder for her to turn over and wouldn't break when she did turn it over.

Tammy's habit of turning over furniture disrupted family life, created disorder, and aggravated her parents. By buying some heavy furniture and nailing other pieces to the wall, Tammy's parents were able to stop her disruptive activity. Another parent described a similar solution to a different behavior problem:

> When Kaylon was 10, he liked to wander all over the house. We belonged to several parent organizations and sometimes had meetings in our house. We needed to know where Kaylon was while we had the meetings, even though we couldn't watch him all the time. I put hooks and eyes high up on all of the doors. Whenever we wanted to close off some rooms, we simply hooked up the doors. Kaylon was free to wander in certain rooms, which enabled us to know where he was and that he was safe.

This father found an unobtrusive way of changing his home to prevent his son's wandering. The hooks and eyes are inexpensive and generally allowed the family to use their home in a normal way. Whenever necessary, the doors could be hooked, which confined Kaylon to those rooms thought to be safe.

COMMON BEHAVIOR PROBLEMS

Although children with autism can exhibit a wide range of problems, these can be conveniently grouped in two broad categories: noncompliance and disruptive behaviors. *Noncompliance* is a technical term for disobedience, or not following parental requests and guidance. Clearly, it is difficult to teach a disobedient child the intended lessons. *Disruptive behaviors* (e.g., temper tantrums) affect more people than noncompliance does; these behaviors can affect the whole family, the classroom, or people in public places. Fear of temper tantrums may cause a family to refrain from engaging in certain activities, particularly if these involve going out in public. Unless the child's disruptive behaviors can be controlled, a family may be prevented from participating in activities of normal family life.

The following sections present examples of how both parents and professionals have dealt with these two types of behavior problems. They are not meant to be an exhaustive list, but are suggestions to stimulate ideas for better managing behavior problems in your own situation.

Noncompliance

To teach new skills or social behaviors, it is most helpful if the child is willing and able to follow instructions. Behaviorists have developed a variety of techniques for improving a child's compliance. Most of those techniques involve basic behavior management techniques described in the preceding section: reinforcement, token systems, time out, adult attention, alteration of the environment, and response cost. It is important to practice techniques that emphasize positive practices rather than punishing the child for his or her disobedience. We often hear that people with autism lack motivation. This may more likely be a matter of finding the right reinforcer rather than giving up on reinforcement. A staff person at a sheltered workshop gave an example of how her persistence paid off:

> Mark, age 26, is a young man who refused to go to his sheltered workshop for weeks. Workshop staff, mental health workers, and other professionals all went to his home to urge him to attend. None of these

people had any success. One staff person came up with the idea of taking Mark to the doughnut store next to the workshop if he would go. Mark got up and dressed himself immediately. There were no further problems getting him to go to the workshop.

This is a clear example of how to use individualized positive reinforcement to motivate compliance. When Mark refused to go to the workshop, the staff tried reasoning with him to persuade him to go. None of these reasons motivated him to go. Once a meaningful reward was found, Mark went to the workshop readily.

A more complex type of positive reinforcement is the use of a token system (Ayllon, Garber, & Allison, 1977; Fjellstedt & Sulzer-Azaroff, 1973). These professionals report cases of handicapped students who refused to follow instructions. Token systems were set up in which students could earn tokens by following instructions. The tokens could be used to buy free time or food rewards and were successful in motivating the students to follow instructions more rapidly. Another symbolic form of reward as a social reinforcement was used in this situation:

> Andrea, age 16, was very difficult to manage in the classroom. She had engaged in a variety of interfering behaviors over the years. For a long time, spanking was the major method of control. Other methods were tried, including a good deal of positive reinforcement. However, none worked as effectively as the "Good Kid Award." Each day that Andrea completed her assignments, she was given a "Good Kid Award."

The "Good Kid Award" is an example of a symbolic social reinforcement like smiley faces, gold stars, or stickers. It is sometimes unexpected for social rewards to be successful with autistic persons, as they usually prefer more tangible rewards such as food. Built into any type of symbolic reward is special praise. Both Andrea's teachers and her parents heaped praise on her whenever she received a "Good Kid Award." This praise, plus her piece of paper, delighted her and helped her to control her behavior more effectively than physical punishment did. A common use of social praise is to increase or decrease the amount of attention paid to a student according to his or her behavior (Schutte & Hopkins, 1970; Wahler, 1969). These researchers trained parents of noncompliant children in basic behavior management techniques. They found that parents' attention was one of the most effective positive reinforcers. Parents learned to increase their attention to their child when he or she was cooperative. With this parental response, the children's behavior improved noticeably.

Wandering is another common concern mentioned by parents of children with autism. It is potentially dangerous and limits both the family's mobility and the child's independence. Children who are unable to listen to their parents' warnings pose a special problem, since they are also often unresponsive to punishment. A group of behaviorists (Barnard, Christophersen, and Wolf, 1977) reported a complex system they devised and found to be successful with three different children in three different families. They set up a point system in which mothers brought point charts to the grocery store. After every 5 minutes, the mother would give her son a point if he hadn't wandered away. If he did wander away, two points were lost. The children were able to trade in their points for candy when they arrived home. The point system proved successful in reducing the wandering behavior. A parent described his method for controlling his son's wandering:

> When Kaylon was younger, he would wander off and be in danger if we did not hold his hand. I told him that I would not hold his hand if he chose to hold mine. If Kaylon let go, I explained that I would be forced to hold his hand. He felt more independent when he initiated the hand holding. Over time we faded out holding hands to having Kaylon hold just one finger. As he got older, hand holding looked inappropriate, so I taught him to hold my sleeve instead. Eventually, he learned to walk next to me without wandering away.

Kaylon's father used a simple but subtle management technique. He recognized his son's stubbornness and his desire to feel more independent. On the other hand, he realized that he could not allow Kaylon to walk by himself, since he would wander away. To solve this dilemma, the father taught Kaylon new ways to stay in touch and at the same time gave Kaylon control over holding his dad's hand. Kaylon felt more important, and his father was able to take him out in public safely.

Disruptive Behavior

Children with autism may exhibit various disruptive behaviors such as temper tantrums, screaming, kicking, hitting, and biting. In most instances, the approach used is illustrated by the icebergs and represented in most of the anecdotes in this volume. The emphasis is on close observation of the incident and knowledge of the child's related behavior history or related medical issues. The disruptive behavior is then related to a problem-solving intervention. In the large majority of cases, this approach is effective. However, in a small percentage of cases or incidents, no underlying cause can be found. Nevertheless, the disruptive behaviors need to be controlled. One method for control developed by behaviorists is time out (Schreibman, 1994). This procedure, described earlier in this chapter, involves removing the child from the environment where the behavior is taking place for a set period of time. When time out is used consistently right after the unacceptable behavior occurs, it is often effective. Parents sometimes use it spontaneously.

> My daughter Faye, who is 8, often screams or makes strange noises when she can't get her way. We began to tell her that when she made these noises, we were going to send her outside. She likes to get a lot of attention and doesn't like to be sent outside. She has learned that going outside is "bad," and therefore she inhibits her noise making when we threaten to send her outside.

Time out will be effective if something in the environment maintains the behavior and if the child dislikes time out. In many cases, a child continues a disruptive behavior because he or she is receiving a great deal of attention for it. Faye's parents recognized this and realized that when Faye screamed, they had to send her someplace where the screaming wouldn't bother them and where Faye wouldn't get any attention for it. They sent her outside, which she did not like, and this effectively decreased her screaming. Having a disruptive child change environments does not need to be used in a punitive way in order to be effective.

> My 4-year-old-son, Bobby, sometimes gets very upset. We found that if we put him outside at these times, he can calm down more quickly than he does inside. The change in environment seems to help him. He is able to be active swinging, sliding, and so on, which helps calm him down.

These parents discovered that removing Bobby from the place where he is upset and sending him outside helps to calm him down. His is not a time-out procedure, but rather a way for calming him down by offering him a chance to engage in alternative behaviors. Outside he is able to be active and can release his anger and frustration. A word of caution should be mentioned here. In offering alternatives, it is important to ask if the crying behavior is being reinforced by letting Bobby go outside every time he cries. If it is, or does not decrease, another approach is needed.

Parents and professionals have found that sometimes behavior problems can be avoided by recognizing the warning signs of disruptive behavior and changing the situation before it occurs. For example, one way to prevent temper tantrums is to teach alternative behaviors for the child to engage in every time he or she begins to get anxious or angry. McLaughlin and Nay (1975) reported a case of how they treated an adolescent woman who pulled her hair when she became nervous. They taught her a relaxation procedure that consisted of listening to pleasant music and carrying out breathing exercises. Whenever she began to pull her hair, she learned to go to her tape player and begin her relaxation tape. This procedure was successful at reducing her hair pulling. One mother described a less complicated procedure she used with her teenage daughter:

> Whenever I awaken Janey, I can tell if it is going to be a bad morning. If she is very sleepy and hard to wake up, she usually has temper tantrums. Janey has repeated this pattern of behavior many mornings, and usually the grumbling, stamping, and throwing things culminate in her refusing to get on the school bus. I tried to deal with this behavior in several ways: driving Janey to school later or punishing her for her bad behavior. Nothing seemed to work. I knew that Janey loved music, especially the Beach Boys. I decided to play one of her tapes if it looked like she was going to have a bad morning. Now the strains of the Beach Boys break up Janey's bad moods and get the morning off to a cheerful start.

Janey's mother learned to recognize the warning signs of her daughter's bad moods. Whenever it was difficult to wake up Janey, it was likely that she would be in a bad mood. By introducing pleasant music, Janey's attention was diverted to something she liked. Such an approach is often effective. It is simpler to prevent a temper tantrum than to cope with it after it reaches full force. A teacher described a procedure she used to redirect a student's attention and avoid temper tantrums:

> Ted is a 6-year-old student in my class who has a tantrum whenever he can't get his way. It seemed that my telling him "yes" or "no" set up a power struggle and led to a big fight. I knew that he was fascinated with lights, so I brought a toy traffic light to class. I taught him that whenever I pushed the green light, he could get what he wanted. Whenever I pushed the red light, he couldn't get what he wanted. He was so fascinated with the light that he obeyed instructions without tantruming.

Both parents and professionals have noted that children are less angry about being told they cannot get something they want when they feel the refusal is given impersonally. Some children follow directions better when they are written, or if they are given as a general rule for everyone rather than as a personal rule for that student. Ted's teacher took advantage of his interest in lights to make giving him instructions more pleasant for him. By using the traffic light to give instructions, she depersonalized the instructions, as if they came from the traffic light rather than from her. Since Ted was fascinated by the light, he obeyed the instructions without a fuss. Sometimes temper tantrums can be avoided by making instructions more clear. One study (Bernal, Duryee, Pruett, & Burns, 1968) reported a child who seemed to tantrum whenever his mother told him to do something. They helped the mother learn to give instructions more clearly and firmly, which reduced the boy's temper tantrums. A parent described one way she avoided her son's temper tantrums:

> Rick has problems being patient and waiting for something he likes. Sometimes he gets so impatient while waiting that he tantrums. Whenever our family is planning a trip, I help him to anticipate it calmly. We set up a calendar and visually mark the time until the trip. Each day we talk about it—what day it is today, how many days until the trip, what he will see there, and so on. This helps him to control his anxiety and to be more patient.

Rich had temper tantrums whenever he had to wait for something he liked. Because of his poor concept of time, he did not understand that "waiting" meant that he would still get what he wanted, although not immediately. His mother used the calendar to provide a visual cue for Rich. The calendar showed him when he would get to go on the trip, which lessened his confusion. This reminded him that he would get to go on the trip and provided him with something he could do in the interim period. Such visual structure has been used to prevent behavior problems with many autistic children (Schopler, Mesibov, & Hearsey, 1995).

Most social activities require following rules. Because autistic children often find it difficult to understand rules, they frequently become upset when forced to obey a rule. A parent provides an example of how she decreased her son's temper tantrums by helping him to understand a rule:

> My son Dick used to tantrum whenever we stopped the car at a stop sign. He loved to look out the window while the car was moving and watch everything we passed. We took him out on walks and showed him what a stop sign was and what it meant. He learned to look at the stop sign, wait, and then cross the street. Now he is able to ride in the car and wait patiently when we stop at a stop sign.

Dick did not understand why his parents were stopping the car, and he became angry whenever they stopped at stop signs. The stop sign didn't mean anything to him. As far as he was concerned they were stopping for no reason. His parents taught him what a stop sign was and how to behave when he saw one. Once he learned this, he became able to wait patiently in the car whenever his parents had to stop at stop signs.

Destructive Behavior

Only a very small proportion of behavior problems are in this category (see Chapter 5). Because of its intensity and/or frequency and duration, destructive behavior presents an imminent danger to the person who exhibits it, to other people, or to property. Severe self-injurious behavior can involve repeated self-inflicted injuries and can produce bleeding, broken bones, or permanent tissue damage. Less serious to the individual, but more dangerous for family and caregivers, are assaultive behaviors that injure others.

The initiating cause is usually unknown but may be due to an enzyme deficiency. In addition, destructive behavior has also been ascribed to neuroanatomical, physiological, or chemical abnormalities; social and environmental deprivation; and a need for stimulation due to sensory deficits. Such behavior occurs more often in institutionalized individuals, but can occasionally appear at home.

Destructive behaviors are usually prevented or treated by the kind of home-grown interventions illustrated in this manual or by the more technical behavior management techniques discussed in this chapter. In the past, when such efforts were not effective, drug therapy and/or aversive therapy techniques were implemented. These should not be used without professional supervision, and even then for limited time periods.

Drug Therapy

There is general professional agreement that no single drug therapy has been found to be effective for autism (Gualtieri, Evans, & Patterson, 1987). Nevertheless, there is evidence that drug therapy is used excessively, especially in institutions. Drugs used to reduce destructive behavior include neuroleptics, barbiturates, stimulants, antianxiety drugs, antidepressants, anticonvulsants, and opiate antagonists. Many of these have negative side effects. Most frequently prescribed are the neuroleptics, which have tardive dyskinesia (a movement disorder) as a negative side effect of long-term usage. Such drugs should be used only for a specifically targeted behavior over a limited time period, with relevant blood tests, and under good medical supervision.

Aversive Therapy Techniques

Aversive therapy techniques to reduce the frequency of a behavior are used as a last resort when all other techniques have failed. They may involve brief (fraction of a second) electric shock delivered to the skin, a disagreeable-tasting substance placed in the mouth or air, water mist, ammonial salts placed briefly under the nose, or tickling. Other behavior reduction treatments involve overcorrection (e.g., cleaning up their own spill and spills made by others), restraints, and those previously discussed.

The use of such aversives is controversial and has resulted in bitter debates among professionals. There is widespread general professional agreement that positive reinforcement or rewards should be used far more frequently than any form of punishment. However, a consensus panel formed by the National Institute of Mental Health (1990) has recommended that such procedures may be used if the clinical situation requires it after appropriate review, and only in the context of a total treatment program. There are some who hope that with the right kind of new research, the day will come when punishment and aversive techniques will no longer be necessary. Fortunately, these most difficult behavior problems occur only rarely.

In the meantime, this manual is dedicated as a celebration of parents and others who have found humane ways of living with autism in their families, and who have found solutions to special problems that at times coincide with the best of our current behavioral science knowledge. This kind of dedicated effort can be an inspiration to all of us, whether we are struggling with child-rearing problems defined by the *Diagnostic and Statistical Manual* or with behavior problems recognized primarily by our own families.

REFERENCES

Ayllon, T., Garber, S. W., & Allison, M. G. (1977). Behavioral treatment of childhood neurosis. *Psychiatry, 40,* 315–322.

Barnard, J. D., Christophersen, E. R., & Wolf, M. M. (1977). Teaching children appropriate shopping behavior through parent training in the supermarket setting. *Journal of Applied Behavior Analysis, 10,* 49–59.

Bernal, M. E., Duryee, J. S., Pruett, H. E., & Burns, B. J. (1968). Behavior modification and the brat syndrome. *Journal of Consulting and Clinical Psychology, 32,* 447–455.

Doleys, D. M., Wells, K. C., Hobbs, S. A., Roberts, M. W., & Cartelli, L. M. (1976). The effects of social punishment on noncompliance: A comparison with timeout and positive practice. *Journal of Applied Behavior Analysis, 9,* 471–482.

Fjellstedt, M., & Sulzer-Azaroff, B. (1973). Reducing the latency of a child responding to instructions by means of a token system. *Journal of Applied Behavior Analysis, 6,* 125–130.

Gualtieri, T., Evans, R. W., & Patterson, D. R. (1987). The medical treatment of autistic people: Problems and side effects. In E. Schopler & G. B. Mesibov (Eds.). *Neurobiological Issues in Autism* (pp. 374–385). New York: Plenum Press.

Haring, T. C., & Kennedy, C. H. (1990). Contextual control of problem behavior in students with severe disabilities. *Journal of Applied Behavior Analysis, 23,* 235–243.

Kanoly, P., & Rosenthal, M. (1977). Training parents in behavior modification: Effects on perceptions of family interactions and deviant children. *Behavior Therapy, 8,* 406–410.

McLaughlin, J. G., & Nay, W. R. (1975). Treatments of trichotillanonia using positive covariants and response cost: A case report. *Behavior Therapy, 6,* 87–91.

Mesibov, G. B. (in press). Division TEACCH: A collaborative model program for service delivery, training, and research for people with autism and related communication handicaps. In M. C. Roberts (Ed.), *Model programs in service delivery in child and family mental health.* New York: Plenum Press.

National Institute of Health. (1990). Consensus development conference statements: Treatment of destructive behaviors in persons with developmental disabilities. *Journal of Autism and Developmental Disorders, 20,* 403–429.

Ruggles, T., & LeBlanc, J. (1985). Behavior analysis procedures in classroom teaching. In A. S. Bellack, M. Heusen, & A. E. Kazdin (Eds.), *International handbook of behavior modification and therapy* (student ed., pp. 353–390). New York: Plenum Press.

Schreibman, L. (1994). General principles of behavior management. In E. Schopler & G. B. Mesibov (Eds.), *Behavioral issues in autism* (pp. 11–38). New York: Plenum Press.

Schopler, E., Mesibov, G. B., & Hearsey, K. (1995). Structured Teaching in the TEACCH system. In E. Schopler & G. B. Mesibov (Eds.), *Learning and Cognition in Autism* (pp. 243–268). New York: Plenum Press.

Schutte, R. C., & Hopkins, B. L. (1970). The effect of teacher attention on following instructions in a kindergarten class. *Journal of Applied Behavior Analysis, 3,* 117–122.

Sulzer-Azaroff, B., & Pollack, M. J. (1985). The modification of child behavior problems in the home. In A. S. Bellack, M. Hensen, & A. E. Kazdin (Eds.), *International handbook of behavior modification and therapy* (student ed. pp. 311–352). New York: Plenum Press.

Wahler, R. G. (1969). Oppositional children: A quest for parental reinforcement control. *Journal of Applied Behavior Analysis, 2,* 159–170.

Wahler, R. G., & Foxx, J. J. (1980). Solitary toy play and time-out: A family treatment package for children with aggressive and oppositional behavior. *Journal of Applied Behavior Analysis, 13,* 23–39.

Weiner, H. (1962). Some effects of response costs upon human operant behavior. *Journal of the Experimental Analysis of Behavior, 5,* 201–208.

9

Community Support

Alice Wertheimer

P revious chapters deal with the special behavior problems generated by autism and how these are resolved within the family. In this chapter, we describe how these problems can be ameliorated through community support and information at the local, state, and national levels.

The resources we present help answer the common questions parents ask about their communities, such as, Who will understand my child, my struggles? Who can I talk to? Who are the sympathetic doctors and dentists? Which are the best schools? Where are the accepting restaurants, playgrounds, and swimming pools? This chapter presents the various ways in which parents can collaborate in their own communities. It is demonstrated that when parents come together as friends to help and support one another, they can successfully advocate for services and create beneficial programs. Finally, we provide an important list of national organizations that offer information and reading materials of special interest to anyone touched by a child with autism.

I am one of the parents who has struggled with many of the personal and practical issues presented in this book. In my experience, the most useful solutions were produced by collaboration with understanding, knowledgeable professionals and with other parents of children with autism. Many of my dearest friendships are those that grew out of the common struggles with autism.

For me, parenting my child with autism has been like parenting my other child—both a blessing and a challenge. It is an experience filled with ups and downs, triumphs and struggles, and most of all, a lot of love.

STARTING OUT ALONE

One of the most overwhelming aspects of being a parent of a child with autism is the risk of intense isolation. Too few family members or friends understand what autism is and how it affects you, your child, and your family. Your child seems so different. You feel so alone.

During the early years of my son's life, we did not live in North Carolina. We had little means of support from local professionals or other parents. Among my saddest memories from that period is of our daily jaunts to the local playground. There my son's activity was limited to walking along the periphery of the playground's fence—focusing exclusively on its symmetrical lines—in a solitary, repetitious pattern, while dozens of toddlers played happily on swings, ropes, and see-saws. I was surrounded by seemingly happy, carefree adults and the sights and sounds of children (except mine) at play. I had never felt more alone.

As hard as they tried and as well-meaning as they were, even close friends and family members provided little consolation to the sadness we felt when coming to terms with our son's diagnosis. As we grappled with the realization that he was not to be the little boy we thought he would be, we simultaneously had to learn everything there was to know about autism. Additionally, we were basically on our own to find the local resources that could assist us. We had to find how to deal with his difficult tantrums, where to find the best speech therapist, what school program was best for him, how to help his older sister understand autism, and how to deal with the countless, difficult daily issues of raising a handicapped child.

I discovered that my best survival mechanism was to connect with other parents of autistic children. It was parents—the actual soldiers in the trenches—who knew the local resources and support services, and had the great ideas! It was parents—those of us randomly thrown together in an ordeal for which we were unprepared—who would help us to deal with autism.

One of the first phone calls I made after learning our son's diagnosis was to a stranger whose name I was given when I asked the doctor for another parent to talk with. I felt the urgency to speak with someone who had already been through this predicament, someone who would know what this pain felt like. I will always remember that conversation as one of the most significant in my life. The other mother's child was only a few years older than mine, so she could relate to everything I was feeling and all the questions I had. But for me the most important part of our talk was hearing that I was not alone, that *someone else* had actually gone through the same moments of intense uncertainty, love, loss, and fear. She told me that one day I would even be able to laugh at the unique humor of autism.

Following my talk with the other mother, I felt that at last, after enduring the painful struggle to figure out what was wrong with our son and then how to help him, I'd found someone who understood. It was evident to me that the key to my survival would be to create effective and caring relationships with other parents and professionals in the autism community.

After moving to North Carolina, where the TEACCH program supports the collaboration between parents and professionals, I joined with other parents of autistic children so that collectively we could share experiences, information, aspirations, and fellowship.

Two resources that developed from this unifying process in the Chapel Hill, North Carolina, area have been of immeasurable value to families of children with autism. These are the *Chapel Hill Area Local Unit* ("CHALU"), a local chapter of the Autism Society of North Carolina, and the *Triangle Autism Resource Guide,* a resource book compiled by a group of mothers affiliated with the Chapel Hill TEACCH clinic. Both are networking tools that could easily be transferred to other regions by parents willing to create and develop their own support systems.

LOCAL UNITS

The resource most in keeping with this book's spirit of parents helping parents is the *local unit.* This grassroots organization has the potential to directly affect the lives of families who have a child with autism. Local units may be any type of community-based group of parents (and interested others) who have in common their children with autism. They may be affiliated with the Autism Society of America or be local units of their state chapters.

In Chapel Hill, we had the advantage of the support of Division TEACCH. Yet parents of children with autism everywhere have the same need to find solutions to the challenges we all face. One of the ideal places to look for those solutions is in our own backyards. The first step in the voyage of advocacy is to locate other parents of children with autism in our own hometowns, school districts, counties, or geographic regions.

Those new to autism may find that there already is a local unit where they live. It may be found by contacting the Autism Society chapter of your state, or calling the national organization—the Autism Society of America—at 1-800-3-AUTISM (or 1-800-328-8476). If there is not a group in your area, you may try to reach other parents by asking at your child's school, doctor's office, early intervention programs, or state agencies. Joining together will empower you and make it easier to deal with the problems autism poses both at home and in the community.

CHAPEL HILL AREA LOCAL UNIT

In Chapel Hill, our local unit, affectionately known as "CHALU" (Chapel Hill Area Local Unit), is a local chapter of the Autism Society of North Carolina, which is our state's chapter of the Autism Society of America. CHALU was founded 3 years ago as part of the process of bringing together local parents who had similar needs and concerns regarding their children with autism.

In 1991, I invited the parents of my son's five classmates to my house to talk about issues concerning our children's education. I was moved by the delight the parents expressed at having the chance to meet one another. That first meeting had the quality of a casual get-together of friends who had a lot in common. We shared anecdotes about our children, discussed personal issues of concern, and then together formulated a strategy for advocating to school administrators for the services our children required. This group of five parents began to meet regularly. At one meeting, we invited the school district's exceptional services director to join us. He was the administrator who had most control over our children's program. Having him with us for a casual evening while we presented him with our concerns, was a compelling technique. Not only did we become better acquainted with him, and he with us, but it also helped us to feel comfortable and effective as a group.

While the core group of five became more effective, my friend Sherry Anscher and I began discussing the powerful potential that this group represented. We thought of many innovative and needed programs that could be put into place if we were able to organize the growing numbers of parents of autistic children (and interested others) in Chapel Hill. We felt that if even our small group of five could have an impact on the school administration, then endless opportunities existed if we could locate and inspire all of the others in the community.

With assistance from our state chapter, The Autism Society of North Carolina, we held a kick-off meeting to determine if there would be enough interest to start a local unit. The state office provided us with their lists of names of potentially interested people in our area as well as with publicity in our local news media. We sent flyers to all of the special education classes in the school district. We invited all of the teachers, doctors, TEACCH and other professionals, neighbors, and friends who might be interested in supporting a local unit. The results far exceeded our expectations! Fifty people attended our first meeting. Everyone present was introduced and had the opportunity to speak about his or her own visions for a local unit. Some of the parents were meeting with other local parents for the first time. Everyone present was in favor of organizing immediately and of becoming an official local unit of our state chapter. We committed ourselves to creating a positive arena for support, service, and friendship. Sherry and I took on the leadership of the group as co-presidents, and several others volunteered to serve as a Board of Directors. The enthusiasm our plans had generated was contagious! Today CHALU is a thriving community organization with more than 50 members.

Administration

CHALU is led by a nine-member Board of Directors headed by a president and operates according to a standard set of bylaws that are based on those of the Autism Society of America. We establish our calendar of events a year in advance, scheduling organizational, informative, advocacy, and social programs. General meetings are held monthly in a log cabin at a local church. This site was arranged by a board member who is a member of the church and takes responsibility for its use. The meetings vary in nature from support, education, information about local resources, guest speaker presentations, and program development ideas. Our Board of Directors meets monthly to discuss plans for future projects and to deal with immediate advocacy issues.

Accomplishments

In only a few years, this fledgling group has achieved substantial goals. The goals are developed for the common good, not merely to satisfy the needs of individual families or children. I believe our group has been successful because of the members' strong desire to work as a team. From this growing sense of camaraderie have blossomed some deep and abiding friendships.

Among CHALU's accomplishments are various recreation programs, a sibling group, a respite program, a monthly newsletter, social events, an educational plan for a middle school class and the development of a Group Home Board. In 1994, we held a full-day conference on Autism and Computers, which drew over 100 attendees.

Programs are funded through membership dues, which are currently $20 annually for parents and $10 for teachers and other professionals.

Some CHALU events have already become annual traditions, such as Appreciation Night, a Halloween family carnival, a December holiday party, a "Summer Splash" event, and a family retreat.

Newsletter

Our members are kept informed via a newsletter, called *The Rainman,* which provides a calendar of coming events as well as an outlet for creativity for family members, teachers, and friends. Everyone is invited to submit artwork and articles for monthly publication. Some children even have regular columns, such as "Matthew's Movie Reviews" and "Paul's Sports Analysis." The newsletter is also a potential source of income for our local unit. *The Rainman* is made possible thanks to the commitment of an editor (currently Mary Anne Rosenman) and because subscriptions are offered free to dues-paying members and by subscription fee to nonmembers.

LOCAL UNIT BASICS

Local units are a vital survival tool for parents of children with autism. But not all communities will develop their local units exactly like CHALU. Each local unit will reflect its own community's character and needs. The groups may be as individual as their members and the locales they represent. Yet, ideally, they serve five distinct purposes: support, education, public relations, advocacy, and services.

Support

The essence of the local unit is its function as a support group. Parents of children with autism generally seek the compassion, understanding, and empathy that only others in the same circumstances can provide. Local units may schedule adequate time throughout the year for general open-discussion meetings that provide talking and listening time. Lists of names and phone numbers of members should be available to everyone. These lists can even provide some detailed information about the members such as ages of children, particular behavior problems, and advocacy interests.

Education

After receiving their child's diagnosis of autism, parents often have nowhere to go to learn more about the disability and the places where they can find help. The local unit may serve as an orientation center for new families in several ways. The unit may have designated members whose role it is to speak to new parents and offer support and understanding. They can have written materials available regarding autism, the local unit and its services, and the resources available in the area. They may develop a resource guide (see the section on the *Triangle Autism Resource Guide*). The local unit may also provide ongoing information in the form of regular meetings with speakers who address a variety of topics.

Public Relations

Because autism is a low-incidence disability, many people are unfamiliar with it. It may be one of the goals of the local unit to make everyone with whom our children come in contact—from the butcher and the baker to neighbors, churches and synagogues, public school teachers, and local government officials—aware of what autism is. Local units can make it their mission to impart to everyone in the community the information needed to recognize and accept children with autism. Members might present programs at schools and other public forums. They can ask local recreation providers to include children with autism in their sports or arts programs. They can address issues of concern on local radio or television stations. The local unit may publish a newsletter and make it available to key community and school leaders. Parents of children with autism should be duly represented on PTA, Exceptional Children Councils, and similar school governance committees. A member of the local unit may be assigned to regularly attend school board meetings and to represent children with autism when issues of concern arise.

Advocacy

Advocacy is a key function of the local unit. Local parents are the ones who best know the schools and programs in the community and the people to contact to access these services. The most useful information about the system may come from parents who have experience using it. Local unit members make the strongest advocates because they understand the advantage presented by their strength in numbers. Schools may be less likely to provide needed services to one child, yet may be more apt to recognize the need when a *group* of parents with similar concerns presents their case. In this way, the local unit supplies a ready-made advocacy group that can spring into action when issues arise.

Services

As the saying goes, "If you want to get anything done, you'll have to do it yourself." This holds true for providing services to families of handicapped children. The local unit serves its most important function when it serves its own members. The member families themselves are directly affected by activities of the local unit. Depending on the needs and wishes of a particular group, local units can organize and provide *for themselves* services such as babysitting, sibling groups, newsletters, telephone hotlines, or any other cooperative efforts.

To be successful, it is critical that the local unit members work as a team—with each person doing what he or she can to achieve goals for the common good. Board members should head up committees that work on specific programs. These programs should serve a wide spectrum of people with autism and their families. *Individuals should keep the entire autism community in mind and create goals accordingly.* Everyone will benefit when the group works together to design services that will suit the needs of all the members.

Guidelines

In summary, the following suggestions may assist others who would like to establish a local unit:

1. Invite parents to meet for an informal, friendly get-together.
2. Include local teachers and other professionals who work with autistic children.
3. Keep the group focused on the common good.
4. Publicize locally through a variety of media.
5. Develop a newsletter for the purpose of keeping informed and as a means of expression and potential income.
6. Obtain assistance from the state chapter of the Autism Society.
7. Start with one goal and increase gradually. Don't expect too much too soon.
8. Don't be afraid to charge a membership fee.
9. Adopt a set of standard bylaws.
10. Have some fun!

Further Information

For more information about forming a local unit, contact the Autism Society of America at 1-800-3-AUTISM, or call your own state's chapter of the Autism Society. For more information about CHALU or to receive a subscription to *The Rainman,* write to:

Maryanne Rosenman
100 Stoneridge Drive
Chapel Hill, North Carolina 27514

TRIANGLE AUTISM RESOURCE GUIDE

Any group of parents gathering together on a regular basis will, on occasion, mention doctors, stores, restaurants, babysitters, and other services that they have used. Mothers of children with autism discuss these same services—but with a different slant. We tend to focus our discussions on the local services that accommodate the special needs of our children. Anyone who has brought his or her young autistic child to a pediatrician, shoe store, or restaurant that was not particularly patient or responsive to special needs children knows that there constantly looms a major potential for disaster. We seek out the least stimulating groceries, the fastest-serving restaurants, the most understanding and knowledgeable doctors, the most kid-friendly shoe stores, the most adaptable summer programs, and so on. In addition, parents of children with autism scour local communities in search of the specialized services our families require, such as speech pathologists, occupational therapists, psychologists, dentists, lawyers, teachers, babysitters, and developmental pediatricians. What better way to find these services than through the referral of another parent?

The Chapel Hill Mother's Group, a TEACCH support group, found that over the years, this kind of resource-swapping had been a vital part of the group's essence. Many of us had found help for our children thanks to recommendations made by our friends while sitting around the Mother's Group table. We wondered if it wouldn't be even more helpful to trade this information in a formal way. It seemed that increasing numbers of families with autistic children were moving to our area, and more children were being diagnosed with autism all the time. So, at the urging of our leader and mentor, Dr. Lee Marcus, we decided to initiate a project that would compile our personal recommendations of services and make them public. The idea was for it to be the publication we mothers wished had been available when our own children were first diagnosed—a kind of "insider's guide" to finding local services for families with autistic children.

The project began by deciding exactly what kind of information we wanted to make available to local families. We felt that there were certain categories of resources that were important to include. In addition, we wanted to provide information about ourselves—the mothers writing the guide. We felt that by publishing a biography about each of us and including information about our children with autism, readers (parents new to autism) would feel a connection with another parent whom they could call for support and information.

The categories we chose, which later made up the guide's Table of Contents, were as follows:

Professional Services
    Diagnosis and Assessment
    Medical and Dental
    Psychological
    Speech and Language
    Occupational and Physical Therapy
    Legal
    Real Estate
Educational Programs
Advocacy and Support
Advocacy Resources
Respite Services
Group Homes
Summer Programs
Recreation
Restaurants and Other Services
Getting Started
Reading List
Autism Bookstore
Mother's Group Biographical Sketches

The biographical sketches were provided by each mother completing a standard form. The form consisted of:

Name/address/phone number
Occupation
Marital status/spouse's name/spouse's occupation
Children's names/children's ages (with indication of child who has autism)
Information about autistic child

School attended/Type of Classroom/School District
Description of child's special interests/abilities
Special problems concerning autistic child
Listing of resources of particular help

The resource guide was in the making for about 2 years. Its creation is a model of the parent–professional collaborative process. The mothers did all of the writing, and the technical support for typing, publishing, and compiling was done by the Chapel Hill TEACCH center and the Autism Society of North Carolina. In fact, Dr. Marcus suggested that the Mother's Group apply for a grant through the Autism Society of North Carolina to offset the costs of publishing the guide. When that grant money was received from the Wake Medical Foundation in Raleigh, we had a small budget with which to cover our typing and copying expenses.

In 1993, the *Triangle Autism Resource Guide* was published. It has been successfully distributed by the Chapel Hill TEACCH center to parents in search of local services and support. In 1994, a series of insert revisions became available for the guide, which is bound in a looseleaf folder.

The resource guide is a tribute to the ideal of parents supporting parents as well as the virtues of the parent–professional collaborative process embodied by Division TEACCH. More than anything, the guide is an example of the possibilities for support and help that parents can provide for one another.

Parents in any community who see the need to formally share resource information could create their own resource guide. The project does not demand tremendous budgets, technical expertise, or fancy packaging. All that is required is a genuine desire to work together with friends who have autism in common to create a product that will benefit everyone.

STEPS TO DEVELOPING A LOCAL RESOURCE GUIDE

In working on the resource guide, the Mother's Group found the following guidelines helpful:

1. Decide on exactly what information you want to share and divide it into specific categories.
2. Assign writing tasks according to categories.

3. Create a standard form for collection of biographical/family sketches. These should contain information about individual group members, their families, and specifics about the individual with autism. Indicate by category the exact behavioral issues the person with autism has faced (for example, toileting problems, eating disorder, obsessions).
4. Assign or hire a coordinator who will compile, edit, type, and keep the project alive.
5. Apply for grants or scholarships through the state chapter or other organization.
6. Hold regularly scheduled work sessions to brainstorm and compile ideas.
7. Determine a target market for the guide. Decide on a price and how to distribute (through local doctors, clinics, schools, developmental centers, local units, and state chapters of the Autism Society).
8. Keep in mind that all information will need to be updated. Build that into the format as well as the product itself (that is use a three-ring binder that can accommodate revisions).
9. Have fun!

RESOURCE LIST
The following resources are of special interest to parents:

Autism Society of America (ASA)
7910 Woodmont Avenue, Suite 650
Bethesda, MD 20814
1-800-3-AUTISM (1-800-328-8476)

The national advocacy organization, ASA is an important first contact for parents new to autism. Founded in 1965, the ASA has several thousand members as well as state and local chapters throughout the United States. New parents can call the ASA on the toll-free line to receive a helpful packet of resource information as well as referrals to local units in their areas.

The Advocate, the ASA's quarterly magazine, offers a wealth of information of current interest.

The ASA holds an annual 4-day conference hosted by a different state chapter each year. The immense magnitude of this conference gives parents and professionals vast opportunities for networking with one another as well as gaining cutting-edge information from the top specialists in the field.

A panel of professional advisers provides the ASA with professional expertise. ASA members have the opportunity to discuss current issues directly with the panel during a dinner meeting at each annual conference. The current panel members are listed below.

Co-chairs
B. J. Freeman, Ph.D.
UCLA School of Medicine
Center for Health Science,
Psychology Department
Los Angeles, California 90024

Luke Y. Tsai, M.D.
Professor and Director
Child and Adolescent Psychiatry
University of Michigan Medical Center
1500 East Medical School Drive
Ann Arbor, Michigan 48109

Panel members
Lois Blackwell, Director
Judevine Center for Autism
9455 Rott Road
St. Louis, Missouri 63127

Doris Bradley, Ph.D.
Department of Speech and Hearing
University of South Mississippi
Hattiesburg, Mississippi 39401

Joel Bregman, M.D.
Emory Autism Resource Center
718 Gatewood Road
Atlanta, Georgia 30322-4990

Donald J. Cohen, M.D., Director
Yale Child Study Center
230 South Frontage Road
New Haven, Connecticut 06510

Mary Coleman, M.D., Director
270 Glenwood Road
Lake Forest, Illinois 60045

Margaret Creedon, Ph.D.
The Therapeutic Day School
800 East 55th Street
Chicago, Illinois 60615

Nancy Dalrymple
2312 Montclair Avenue
Bloomington, Indiana 47401

Anne Donnellan, Ph.D.
University of Wisconsin
Center Education Research
1025 West Johnson, Room 570
Madison, Wisconsin 53706

Glen Dunlap, Ph.D.
Department of Child and Family Studies
Early Childhood Learning Center
University of South Florida
13301 Bruce B. Downs Boulevard
Tampa, Florida 33612

William L. E. Dussault, Esq.
Sweet and Dussault
219 East Galer Street
Seattle, Washington 98102

Judith E. Favell, Ph.D.
Au Clair Palms
28308 Churchill Smith Lane
Mount Dora, Florida 32757

Temple Grandin, Ph.D.
2918 Silver Plume Drive, #C3
Fort Collins, Colorado 80526

June Groden, Ph.D., Director
Groden Center for Autism
86 Mount Hope Avenue
Providence, Rhode Island 02906

Paul Hardy, M.D.
Hardy Healthcare Associates, PC
62 Derby Street
Hingham, Massachusetts 02043-3718

Edna R. Herron
3121 South Heather Court
Springfield, Missouri 65804

David Holmes, Ed.D., Executive Director
Eden Family of Programs
One Logan Drive
Princeton, New Jersey 08540

William R. Jenson, Ph.D.
Graduate School of Education
327 Milton Bennion Hall
Salt Lake City, Utah 84112

Lorna Jean King
4626 East Desert Cove
Phoenix, Arizona 85028

Gary LaVigna, Ph.D., Director
Institute for Applied Behavior Analysis
5777 West Century Boulevard, #590
Los Angeles, California 90045

Bennett L. Leventhal, M.D.
University of Chicago
Department of Psychiatry

5841 South Maryland Avenue, MC3077
Chicago, Illinois 60637

Ogden Lindsey, Ph.D.
Route 1, Box 157
Lawrence, Kansas 66049

Andrew D. Maltz, Ph.D.
Groose Pointe Center
15224 Kercheval
Grosse Point Park, Michigan 48230

Ralph Maurer, M.D., Associate Professor
Children's Mental Health Unit
Box J-234, JHMHC
University of Florida
Gainesville, Florida 32610

Gary B. Mesibov, Ph.D., Director
TEACCH Administration and Research
310 Medical School, Wing E
CB #7180
University of North Carolina
Chapel Hill, North Carolina 27599-7180

Robert J. Reichler, M.D., Director
2150 North 107th Street, Suite 200
Seattle, Washington 98103

Bernard Rimland, Ph.D., Director
Autism Research Institute
4182 Adams Avenue
San Diego, California 92216

Edward Ritvo, M.D.
UCLA School of Medicine
Center for Health Science
Psychology Department
Los Angeles, California 90024

Frank Robbins, Ph.D.
55 Segur Lane
Belchertown, Massachusetts 01007

Eric Schopler, Ph.D., Founder/Co-Director
TEACCH Administration and Research
310 Medical School, Wing E
CB #7180
University of North Carolina
Chapel Hill, North Carolina 27599-7180

Ruth Christ Sullivan, Ph.D.
Autism Services Center
605 Ninth Street
P.O. Box 507
Huntington, West Virginia 25710

Harry Wright, M.D.
Box 12474
Columbia, South Carolina 29211

The following states and cities have local chapters of the ASA as of
February 1994. For more specific and current information, call the ASA
at 1-800-3-AUTISM (1-800-328-8476).

Alabama	Carmel
Birmingham	Chula Vista
Huntsville	Covina
Magnolia	Escondido
	Kerman
Arizona	Lake Elsinor
Phoenix	Long Beach
Tucson	Oakdale
	Rocklin
California	Sacramento
Alamo	Santa Barbara
Anaheim	Santa Rosa
Belmont	

Sherman Oaks
Sunnyvale

Colorado
Littleton

Connecticut
Fairfield
Ivorytown
Middlebury
Milford
West Suffield
Woodberry

Delaware
Newark

Florida
Coral Springs
Jacksonville
Lakeland
North Miami Beach
Orlando
Sarasota
St. Petersburg
Temple Terrace
Wellington

Georgia
Atlanta

Hawaii
Honolulu

Illinois
Charleston
Elk Grove
Eureka
Fox Lake

Highland Park
Hinsdale
Homewood
Lombard
Park Forest

Indiana
Crown Point
Goshen
Ft. Wayne
Lafayette
New Richmond
Terre Haute

Iowa
Bettendorf
Cedar Rapids
Council Bluffs
Dubuque
Sioux City

Kansas
Andover
La Cygne
Overland

Kentucky
Henderson
Pewee Valley

Louisiana
Baton Rouge
Gretna
Houma
Lafayette
Lake Charles
Metaire
Monroe

Maine
Gardiner

Maryland
Baltimore
Bel Air
Berwyn Heights
Gleneig
Pasadena
Rockville
Smithsburg
Towson

Massachusetts
Auburn
Longmeadow
Wellesley

Michigan
Detroit
Grand Blanc
Grand Rapids
Holt
Jackson
Kalamazoo
Lansing
Macomb
Marquette
Midland
Muskegon
Otsego
Saginaw
Traverse City
West Bloomfield
Whitmore Lake

Minnesota
Minneapolis

Missouri
Arnold
Aurora
Greenwood

Mississippi
Long Beach

Montana
Billings

Nebraska
Lincoln

Nevada
Las Vegas
Reno

New Hampshire
Concord

New Jersey
Edgewater Park
Island Heights
Lawrenceville
Millville
Neptune
Point Pleasant
Princeton
Ringwood

New Mexico
Albuquerque

New York
Bronx
Brooklyn
Fairport
Huntington
Holliswood

Kingston
New York
Yonkers

North Carolina
Autism Society of North Carolina
With local units in each of the
following TEACCH regions:
Asheville
Chapel Hill
Charlotte
Greensboro
Greenville
Wilmington

Ohio
Athens
Beaver Creek
Boardman
Cincinnati
Dublin
Fairlawn
Macedonia
Toledo

Oklahoma
Oklahoma City
Tulsa

Oregon
Salem

Pennsylvania
Allentown
Drexel Hill
Erie
Irwin
Johnstown

Lancaster
New Castle
Monroeville
Tunkhonnock

Puerto Rico
Hato Rey

Rhode Island
Barrington

South Carolina
Effingham

South Dakota
Elk Point
Midland

Tennessee
Memphis
Nashville

Texas
Arlington
Austin
Flower Mound
Harlingen
Laredo
Lubbock
Missouri City
San Antonio
Whitehouse

Utah
Salt Lake City

Virginia
Hampton
Norfolk
Portsmouth

Richmond
Vienna

Washington
Nine Mile Falls
Seattle

West Virginia
Beckley
Clarksburg

Huntington
Tinsburg

Wisconsin
Appleton
Green Bay
Greendale
Madison
New Lisbon

AUTISM SOCIETY OF NORTH CAROLINA (ASNC)
3300 Woman's Club Drive
Raleigh, North Carolina 27612-4811
(919) 571-8555
1-800-442-2762 (NC only)
(919) 571-7800 (Fax)

The Autism Society of North Carolina (ASNC) is dedicated to the education and welfare of children and adults with autism and their families across North Carolina. Because of the unique collaborative relationship among the North Carolina state legislature, the University of North Carolina (as represented by Division TEACCH), and parents, ASNC is able to offer a full range of services and programs to families in the state. These include the oldest and largest summer camp of its kind, residential development, vocational placement, and statewide advocacy support.

ASNC facilitates local units throughout the state that unite parents, professionals, and interested others on a community level.

ASNC, a state chapter of the Autism Society of America (ASA), publishes a newsletter six times per year and holds a one-day annual conference in the fall.

ASNC offers the nation's largest bookstore featuring selections about autism. Orders can be placed by mail or phone. Write or call for the latest catalog.

The ARC (Association for Retarded Citizens)
500 East Border Street, Suite 300
Arlington, TX 76010
1-800-433-5255

This advocacy organization supports efforts on the national level as well as on local levels for all persons with developmental disabilities. The ARC is a beneficial resource for parents of children with autism who would like to unite with other parents of handicapped children in their communities. Call the national office on the toll-free line for the chapter nearest you.

There are many resources available to families of persons with autism outside of the United States. Due to the variability and frequent changes among international contact groups, it is best to call the Autism Society of America, at 1-800-3-AUTISM, for the most current information.

READING MATERIAL

Newsletters and Journals

This is a sampling of newsletters and journals available on a local, state, and national level. It is by no means a comprehensive listing. Many state and local chapters throughout the United States publish informative newsletters. For more information, contact the Autism Society of America at 1-800-3-AUTISM.

The Advocate*

Newsletter of the Autism Society of America. Features information about national activities as well as local chapter activities. Also notifies members of ASA business and presents a variety of information about autism, treatments, and current research. Especially useful book reviews and information exchange sections.

> To subscribe: Free to members. There are a variety of membership categories, starting at $12.50.
> Contact: Autism Society of America
> 7910 Woodmont Avenue, Suite 650
> Bethesda, Maryland 20814
> 1-800-3-AUTISM or (301) 657-0881

*Indicates that the author/editor is a parent.

ASNC Newsletter
Newsletter of the Autism Society of North Carolina. Features information about ASNC activities and services, as well as current local, state, and national resources.

> To subscribe: Free to members. A variety of membership categories are available, starting at $10.00.
> Contact: Autism Society of North Carolina
>   3300 Woman's Club Drive
>   Raleigh, North Carolina 27612
>   (919) 571-8555

Autism Research Review International*
This is the quarterly publication of the Autism Research Institute, directed by Bernard Rimland, Ph.D., a psychologist and parent of an adult son who has autism. Features a review of biomedical and educational research in the field of autism and related disorders. Contains interesting commentaries by parents regarding their experiences with various treatments.

> To subscribe: 4 issues, $16.00
> Contact: Autism Research Review International
>   4182 Adams Avenue
>   San Diego, California 92116

Focus on Autistic Behavior
Published bimonthly by Pro-Ed, this more scholarly publication offers a calendar of upcoming professional conferences as well as an in-depth look at specific research topics in the autism field.

> Contact: PRO-ED, Inc.
>   8700 Shoal Creek
>   Austin, Texas 78758

The MAAP*
This unique and family-oriented newsletter features interesting letters and discussion articles about "More Able People with Autism." In an easy to read manner, Susan Moreno chats with her readers about issues of concern to high-functioning people with autism and their families. *The MAAP* offers creative works by individuals with autism.

To subscribe: $8.00 annually
Contact: Susan J. Moreno
             The MAAP
             P.O. Box 524
             Crown Point, Indiana 46307

Parents' Newsletter on Special Education Law*
Specialized newsletter written for the parents and interested others of
children with disabilities, it features current federal laws applicable to
special education. Written for the layperson, this bimonthly newsletter
is especially beneficial to parents interested or involved in school
advocacy. Published by Edward Bedford, an attorney who is also the
parent of a child with autism.

To subscribe: 6 issues, $29.00
             12 issues, $49.00
Contact: Parents' Newsletter on Special Education Law
             P.O. Box 4571
             Chapel Hill, NC 27515-4571

POAC Press**
Newsletter of the New Jersey Shore Area chapter of the ASA, called
"Parents of Autistic Children." Focuses on local unit activities as well
as up-to-date resources on local, state, and national levels. Parent–
professional input.

To subscribe: Members of local unit, or by special request.
Contact: Carole Tonks
             POAC
             1637 Bay Avenue
             Point Pleasant, New Jersey 08742

The Rainman*
Newsletter of the Chapel Hill Area Local Unit of the Autism Society of
North Carolina. Features local unit activities and local school news.
Upbeat and supportive, this publication is a forum for the local units'
member families. It offers creative submissions by children with autism
and their siblings. Some resource information on a broader scale is also
presented. Published monthly.

To subscribe: $12.00 per year
Contact: Maryanne Rosenman
               100 Stoneridge Drive
               Chapel Hill, North Carolina 27514

The Wake Warbler*
The monthly newsletter of the Wake County Unit of the Autism Society of North Carolina. Features activities of the local unit and local classrooms, and some resource information on a broader scale.

To subscribe: Members of local unit, or by special request.
Contact: Thea Gardner
               1632 Pricewood Lane
               Apex, North Carolina 27502

Books
All of the following books are available from the Autism Society of North Carolina. For ordering information, contact Mr. Jim Person by phone at (919) 571-8555, or by fax at (919) 571-7800.

Fiction
Family Pictures by Sue Miller

Inside Out (1984) by Ann M. Martin

Joey and Sam (1993) by Illana Katz and Edward Ritvo

Kristy and the Secret of Susan (1990) by Ann M. Martin

Nonfiction
The "A" Book: A Collection of Writings from The Advocate (1992, revised)

Activities for Developing Pre-Skill Concepts in Children with Autism (1987) by Toni Flowers

After the Tears (1987) by Robin Simons

The Artistic Autistic (1992) by Toni Flowers

Aspects of Autism: Biological Research (1988), edited by Lorna Wing

Autism (1992) by Richard L. Simpson and Paul Zionts

Autism and Asperger Syndrome (1991) by Uta Frith

Autism Primer: Twenty Questions and Answers by the Autism Society of North Carolina (ASNC)

Autism . . . Nature, Diagnosis and Treatment (1989), edited by Geraldine Dawson

Autism: A Practical Guide for Those Who Help Others (1990) by John Gerdtz and Joel Bregman

Autism: Explaining the Enigma (1989) by Uta Frith

Autism: Identification, education, and Treatment (1992), edited by Dianne Berkell

Autism Society of NC Camp Operational Manual (1993) by the Autism Society of North Carolina (ASNC)

Autism Treatment Guide (1993) by Elizabeth K. Gerlach

Autistic Adults at Bittersweet Farms (1991), edited by Norman S. Giddan and Jane J. Giddan

Autistic Children by Lorna Wing

Avoiding Unfortunate Situations by Dennis Debbaudt

Beyond Gentle Teaching by John J. McGee and Frank J. Menolascino

The Biology of the Autistic Syndromes (2nd ed., 1992) by Christopher Gillberg and Mary Coleman

The Boy Who Couldn't Stop Washing: The Experience and Treatment of Obsessive-Compulsive Disorder (1989) by Judith Rapaport

Brothers and Sisters: A Special Part of Exceptional Families (2nd ed., 1993) by Thomas H. Powell and Peggy Arenhold Ogle

Brothers, Sisters and Special Needs (1990) by Debra J. Lobato

Case Studies in Autism (1990) by Cheryl D. Seifert

Children Apart (1974) by Lorna Wing

Children with Autism (1989), edited by Michael Powers

Circles of Friends (1989) by Robert and Martha Perske

Community-Based Curriculum (1989) by Mary A. Falvey

The Curriculum System: Success as an Educational Outcome (2nd ed., 1992) by Carol Gray

Detecting Your Hidden Allergies (1988) by William G. Crook

Developing a Functional and Logitudinal Plan (1989) by Nancy Dalrymple

Diagnosis and Treatment of Autism (1989), edited by Christopher Gillberg

Disability and the Family (1989) by H. Rutherford Turnbull, III, Ann Turnbull, G. J. Bronicki, Jean Ann Summers, and Constance Roeder-Gordon

The Early Intervention Dictionary (1993) by Jeanine Coleman

Educating All Students in the Mainstream of Regular Education (1989), edited by Susan and William Stainback and Marsha Forest

Emergence: Labeled Autistic (1986)* by Temple Grandin

Enhancing Communication in Individuals with Autism Through the Use of Pictures and Words (1989) by Michelle G. Winner

Estate Planning for Families of Persons with Disabilities by Susan Hartley, John Stewart, and Margo Tesch

Facilitated Communication Technology Guide (1993) by Carol Lee Berger

Functional School Activities (1989, revised) by Barbara Porco

Growing Towards Independence by Learning Functional Skills and Behaviors (1989) by Parbara Porco

Handbook of Autism and Pervasive Developmental Disorders (1987), edited by Donald Cohen, Anne Donnellan, and Rhea Paul

Hearing Equals Behavior (1993) by Guy Berard, M.D.

Helpful Responses to Some of the Behaviors of Individuals with Autism (1992) by Nancy Dalrymple

Helping People with Autism Manage Their Behavior (1990, revised) by Nancy Dalrymple

Holistic Interpretation of Autism (1990) by Cheryl D. Seifert

How They Grow (1981) by the Autism Society of America

How to Qualify for Social Security Disability (1992) by David A. Morton, III, M.D.

How to Teach Autistic and Severely Handicapped Children (1981) by Robert L. Koegel and Laura Schreibman

How to Treat Self-Injurious Behavior (1980) by Judith E. Favell and James W. Greene

Infantile Autism (1964, revised 1986)* by Bernard Rimland

Introduction to Autism: A Self Instruction Module (1992, revised) by the Indiana Resource Center for Autism

Laughing and Loving with Autism (1993)* edited by R. Wayne Gilpin

Learning Self-Care Skills (1991) by Valerie DePalma and Marci Wheeler

Learning to Be Independent and Responsible (1989) by Nancy Dalrymple

Let Community Employment Be the Goal for Individuals with Autism (1992) by Joanne Suomi, Lisa Ruble, and Nancy Dalrymple

Let Me Hear Your Voice (1993)* by Catherine Maurice*Letting Go* (1993)* by Connie Post

Mixed Blessings (1989)* by William and Barbara Christopher

My Autobiography (1986)* by David Miedzianik

News From the Border (1993)* by Jane Taylor McDonnell and Paul McDonnell

Nobody Nowhere (1992)* by Donna Williams

A Parent's Guide to Autism (1993) by Charles A. Hart

Please Don't Say Hello (1976) by Phyllis Teri Gold

The Professional's Guide to Estate Planning for Families of Individuals with Disabilities (1993) by Susan Hartley and John Stewart

Reaching the Autistic Child (1973, reprinted 1993) by Martin A. Kozloff

Reading (1989, revised) by Barbara Porco

Record Book for Individuals with Autism (1990) by Nancy Dalrymple

Relaxation (1978) by Joseph R. Cautela and June Groden

Russell Is Extra Special by Charles Amenta, III* (1992)

Seasons of Love: Seasons of Loss (1992) by Connie Post

Sex Education: Issues for the Person with Autism (1991) by Nancy Dalrymple

The Sibling (1992) by Barbara Azrialy

The Siege (1982) by Clara Claiborne Park*

Silent Words (1992) by Margaret Eastham, edited by Anne Grice

The Social Story Book (1993) by Carol Gray

Solving the Puzzle of Your Hard to Raise Child (1987) by William Crook with Laura Stevens

Somebody Somewhere (1994) by Donna Williams*

Some Interpersonal Social Skill Objectives and Teaching Strategies for People with Autism (1992) by Nancy Dalrymple

Soon Will Come the Light (1994) by Thomas S. McKean*

The Sound of a Miracle (1991) by Annabel Stehli*

Steps to Independence (1989) by Bruce Baker and Alan Brightman

Teaching Developmentally disabled Children: The Me Book (1981) by O. Ivar Lovaas

Theories of Autism (1990) by cheryl D. Seifert

There's a Boy in Here (1992) by Judy Barron and Sean Barron*

Toileting (1991, revised) by Nancy Dalrymple and Margaret Boarman

Toward Supported Employment (1988) by James F. Gardner, Michael S. Chapman, Gary Donaldson, and Solomon G. Jacobson

Turning Every Stone (1990) by Phyllis Haywood Lambert*

The Ultimate Stranger: The Autistic Child (1974) by Carl Delacato

Until Tomorrow: A Family Lives with Autism (1988) by Dorothy Zietz*

When Slow Is Fast Enough (1993) by Joan F. Goodman

When Snow Turns To Rain (1993) by Craig Schulzes*

Winter's Flower (1992) by Ranae Johnson*

The Wild Boy of Aveyron (1976) by Harlan Lane

The Yeast Connection (3rd ed., 18th printing, 1992) by William Crook

TEACCH BOOKS AND VIDEOS
TEACCH books are available by contacting Plenum Publishing Corporation at 233 Spring Street, New York, New York 10013-1578. The only exception is *Childhood Autism Rating Scale (CARS),* which can be ordered from Western Psychological Services at 12031 Wilshire Boulevard, Los Angeles, California 90025, or by calling 1-800-648-8857. TEACCH videos may be obtained through the Health Sciences Consortium, 201 Silver Cedar Court, Chapel Hill, North Carolina 27514, or by calling (919) 942-8731.

Books
Adolescents and Adult Psychoeducational Profile (AAPEP) (vol. IV, 1988) by Gary Mesibov, Eric Schopler, Bruce Schaffer, and Rhoda Landrus

Autism in Adolescents and Adults (1983), edited by Eric Schopler and Gary Mesibov

Behavioral Issues in Autism (1994) by Eric Schopler and Gary B. Mesibov

Childhood Autism Rating Scale (CARS) (1988) by Eric Schopler, Robert J. Reichler, and Barbara Rochen Renner

Communication Problems in Autism (1985), edited by Eric Schopler and Gary Mesibov

Diagnosis and Assessment in Autism (1988), edited by Eric Schopler and Gary Mesibov

The Effects of Autism on the Family (1984), edited by Eric Schopler and Gary Mesibov

High-Functioning Individuals with Autism (1992), edited by Eric Schopler and Gary Mesibov

Learning and Cognition in Autism (1995) by Eric Schopler and Gary B. Mesibov

Neurobiological Issues in Autism (1987), edited by Eric Schopler and Gary Mesibov

Preschool Issues in Autism (1993) by Eric Schopler, Mary Van Bourgondien, and Marie Bristol

Psychoeducational Profile—Revised (PEP-R) (Vol. 1, 1990) by Eric Schopler, Robert Reichler, Ann Bashford, Margaret D. Lansing, and Lee Marcus

Social Behavior in Autism (1986), edited by Eric Schopler and Gary Mesibov

Teaching Activities for Autistic Children (Vol. 3, 1983) by Eric Schopler, Margaret Lansing, and Leslie Waters

Teaching Spontaneous Communication to Autistic and Communication Handicapped Children (1989) by Linda Watson, Catherine Lord, Bruce Schaffer, and Eric Schopler

Teaching Strategies for Parents and Professionals (Vol. 2, 1980) by Eric Schopler, Robert Reichler, and Margaret Lansing

Videos

Adolescents and Adults with Autism

Autism Services with Division TEACCH

TEACCH Philosophy

TEACCH Program for Parents

TEACCH Program for Teachers

Training Module for the Childhood Autism Rating Scale (CARS)
   Demonstration Demonstration tape
   Practice tape

Training Module for the Psychoeducational Profile (PEP)
   Scoring the PEP: Training tape
   Scoring the PEP: Test tape
   An Individualized Education Program

Index